"From his reflections ⟨ ...⟩ ɪs a
motorcyclist, Joerg Riɛ ... ɹan
our location—it can change our hearts and transform us from tourists to
advocates for justice and peace."
Brian D. McLaren, author, speaker and activist

"Many of us love to travel. But few consider that traveling from one place
to another, whether as tourist, pilgrim, migrant, refugee, vagabond or even
prophet, matters in our relationships with God and others. Joerg Rieger
has shown here that travel is a key theological category in Scripture. He
rightly shows us that a theology of the road, which challenges the status
quo and takes into account power differentials, is crucial for compre-
hending God, ourselves, and our sisters and brothers—on whatever road
we might encounter them."
Kay Higuera Smith, professor of biblical and religious studies,
Azusa Pacific University

"The world's population is becoming increasingly mobile. Whether one
travels for pleasure or business or is compelled to move from one part of
the world to another in search of a better life, there seem to be more and
more people leaving their places of origin in search of something different,
perhaps even something better. Joerg Rieger's book *Faith on the Road* explores the complexity of faith, identity, economics and social justice
through the lens of travel. This is a superbly written volume that approaches these complex issues in a thorough and helpful manner. What I
have read has changed how I think about travel, migration and faith. I
highly recommend this book!"
Dion A. Forster, senior lecturer in systematic theology and ethics,
Stellenbosch University, South Africa

"'God looks different from the dusty roads of Galilee than from the safety
of the temple in Jerusalem.' God also looks different from the difficult
journeys of immigration, legal or illegal, than from the safe and comfortable trips on business or tourism. This book offers us an important
theological reflection on travel, which has become a mark of our glo-
balized world, stimulating us to rethink the meaning and role of Christian
faith today."
Jung Mo Sung, professor, Methodist University, São Paulo, Brazil

FAITH ON THE ROAD

A SHORT THEOLOGY OF
TRAVEL & JUSTICE

JOERG RIEGER

Foreword by Rev. Alexia Salvatierra

IVP Academic

An imprint of InterVarsity Press
Downers Grove, Illinois

InterVarsity Press
P.O. Box 1400, Downers Grove, IL 60515-1426
ivpress.com
email@ivpress.com

Revised edition ©2015 by Joerg Rieger

First edition published by Fortress Press under the title Traveling, *© 2011*

InterVarsity Press® is the book-publishing division of InterVarsity Christian Fellowship/USA®, a movement of students and faculty active on campus at hundreds of universities, colleges and schools of nursing in the United States of America, and a member movement of the International Fellowship of Evangelical Students. For information about local and regional activities, visit intervarsity.org.

Scripture quotations, unless otherwise noted, are from the New Revised Standard Version of the Bible, copyright 1989 by the Division of Christian Education of the National Council of the Churches of Christ in the USA. Used by permission. All rights reserved.

While any stories in this book are true, some names and identifying information may have been changed to protect the privacy of individuals.

Cover design: Cindy Kiple
Interior design: Beth McGill
Images: dark grunge background: © santosha/iStockphoto
*   bicycle wheel: © boschettophophotography/iStockphoto*

ISBN 978-0-8308-4096-0 (print)
ISBN 978-0-8308-9949-4 (digital)

Printed in the United States of America ∞

Library of Congress Cataloging-in-Publication Data

A catalog record for this book is available from the Library of Congress.

P	20	19	18	17	16	15	14	13	12	11	10	9	8	7	6	5	4	3	2	1
Y	32	31	30	29	28	27	26	25	24	23	22	21	20	19	18	17	16	15		

*The world is a book, and those who
do not travel read only one page.*

ATTRIBUTED TO AUGUSTINE

Contents

Foreword

Rev. Alexia Salvatierra

MORE THAN THIRTY YEARS AGO, I had the opportunity to observe the first congressional elections in the Philippines in twenty years under the dictatorial government of Ferdinand Marcos. This two-week experience led to several years of visiting, residing and working in Manila. During my time in the Philippines, I wore multiple hats—from working as a chaplain in the National Children's Hospital and St. Luke's Episcopal Hospital while obtaining my one-year certification in clinical pastoral education to teaching seminary to coleading a project with poor urban squatter women to participating in the Christian wing of the broader movement for justice. I witnessed firsthand the actual martyrdom of colleagues in ministry working for human rights and social justice. This experience was truly and deeply transformative.

Dr. Rieger's insights on the spiritual power of travel ring true. It certainly did challenge many of my assumptions, throw me into the "shock of the sacred" and teach me that the most important question was not whether "God was on my side" but whether I was on God's side. One of my occasional tasks for the Philippine movement was to lead immersion trips in which clergy and congregations from the United States and Europe experienced the suffering of the Filipino people under the Marcos tyranny as well as the initiatives working against it. I saw how possible it was for short-term mission travelers to unconsciously avoid transformation and how important it was to help them understand the roots of the suffering they encountered as well as the role their countries played in creating and sustaining injustice. The success of our efforts was largely dependent on creating a different kind of relationship between the Filipinos and the visitors, one in which the power differentials were recognized and intentionally confronted. In the process we experienced over and over again the miracle of solidarity in which Jesus meets us in and through the oppressed.

Faith on the Road is an important book for anyone seeking to take full advantage of the opportunity travel presents for spiritual transformation. Travel helps awaken the church to our call to be sojourners and reveals the strategies most useful for teaching us a way of being that is "not conformed to the ways of this world." *Faith on the Road* is provocative. Dr. Rieger makes statements that may be difficult for many of us, but I have found that struggling with these ideas is fruitful for learning and growth. Through *Faith on the Road*, the God of the exodus, the wanderers and the pilgrims met me in this struggle in new and refreshing ways.

Get ready to be taken somewhere new.

Preface

MILLIONS OF PEOPLE TRAVEL EVERY DAY, for what seem to be millions of reasons. Some travel for pleasure, others for work and education, and many more travel in order to find a better life. In the United States, even those who do not travel far frequently find themselves on the move. "Americans still move around more than anyone else in the world," read a recent headline; US citizens are on par only with conflict-torn countries like Iraq.[1] Twenty-four percent of Americans reported moving away from their place of residence in the past five years.

In this book, the question is what we can learn from these different forms of travel and what the lessons for faith in the Christian and related Jewish traditions might be, realizing that many of these faith traditions took shape on the road. From Adam and Eve to the book of Revelation there is movement, from the exile from Eden to the search for the heavenly Jerusalem. People of faith who let themselves be inspired by this movement, who are willing to learn from others and from mistakes made in the process, are well-positioned to make a difference in the world, not only at home but also around the globe.

In our time different types of travel have developed, creating new opportunities and challenges. In vagabonding, mostly young people leave their places of home to explore the world, seeking adventure and broader horizons. Migration is a very different type of travel in which people leave their places of home for reasons of need and survival. Pilgrimages constitute yet another kind of travel—some are tied up with deep religious quests and others are indistinguishable from tourism, which constitutes one of the biggest travel movements of all time. These types of travel may seem to have little in common at first sight. Yet as we explore them each in turn, we will see what various travelers can learn from each other and what even those staying at home can glean.

I write this book as someone who has learned a great deal on the road. Travel is woven into my life in many ways, the result of a lifelong wanderlust. I grew up in a different country thousands of miles from where I live now. I have traveled to many countries in both the Northern and the Southern Hemispheres. I have traveled for pleasure, for work and out of sheer necessity. Moreover, I have had the opportunity to travel in many different ways: some trips have been self-propelled on land and water, some have been by car and increasingly by motorcycle, and many have taken place by means of public transportation, especially commercial airlines in recent decades.

Traveling with different groups of various backgrounds has made a dramatic difference in my journeys. I have also enjoyed many more travels with my wife, Rosemarie Henkel-Rieger, and later with our twin daughters, Helen and Annika, now travelers in their own right. My wife and daughters were international travelers at an age when I had never left Europe and I am grateful that they always contributed to broadening my horizons. Traveling has helped us all to develop a healthy interest in others and in the world, while keeping us focused on what really matters. I am convinced that our lives would have turned out very differently had we stayed home or traveled merely in the bubbles that privilege affords to some of us.

Finally, I write this book not merely as a traveler but as a Christian theologian who is convinced that travel is an inextricable part of our

Jewish and Christian traditions and our varied experiences with the divine. What concerns me is that this role has for the most part been underappreciated, resulting in perspectives that are not only too narrow but seriously skewed. As we embark on the journey together, broader visions and more hopeful perspectives start to emerge.

The insights of this book grow out of relationships established on the road as well as at home. I am grateful to all who in their own ways contributed to help me see things more clearly, particularly to those who posed challenges along the way, intentionally and unintentionally. After all, the most profound learning often takes place when we are pushed outside of our comfort zones. It would be impossible to name the many individuals who have left their imprints on this project. This project will always remain indebted to them, as names on the covers of books can never tell the whole story.

I am also grateful for publishers and editors who joined the journey at various points. An earlier and shorter version of this book appeared in the series Christian Explorations of Everyday Living, published by Fortress Press, and was translated into Portuguese, Chinese and Korean, where it took on lives of its own. Special thanks to David Congdon of InterVarsity Press for his vision and valuable suggestions in the process of expanding and continuing the project.

Introduction

IN THIS BOOK I ARGUE that Christianity is not primarily a matter of pews and buildings; Christianity is a matter of the road. Two examples can help us get started: in the book of Acts, Christians are called "people of the Way," which is the way of Jesus Christ. In the Gospels, Jesus' life and ministry takes place on the road, and his call is "Follow me." Even when his followers return to their homes they remain in motion, like the disciples who return to Galilee after the resurrection only to be sent out again by Jesus, who promises to be on the road with them (Mt 28:16-20).

For all the traveling activity in our religious traditions that we will examine in the following chapters, it is strange that religion is often treated as a static thing. Communities of faith tend to locate themselves in buildings, some confusing the church with the building itself. In this case, "going to church" means going to a building rather than being part of a particular community. As a result it never occurs to such communities to pay attention to what is happening outside of their buildings, in their neighborhoods, in their cities or in the world. For years the motto of one of the largest Methodist churches in Dallas, Texas, was, "Where the difference is worth the distance."

Church seems to be what happens inside a building; outside is the world, which does not concern us much except when there is an opportunity for us to pull it into the church and assimilate it. Not surprisingly, one of the most popular mission strategies in many places around the world continues to be "bring a friend Sunday." Going to where the people are is not the norm for this type of Christianity and is often left to the specialists: missionaries, evangelists and young people who sign up for short-term mission trips. Have we lost our ability to think outside the ecclesial box?

According to popular opinion, "sitting in church" is the core activity of the Christian faith. In most worship services this sitting is interrupted only by standing in place. In this context, turning to one's neighbors in the pews for ritualized activities may be an improvement over sitting or standing, but it is still not enough. How do we help people of faith understand that God is at work not only in the church and among those who share the faith but also outside of it in the world? And how do we develop broader perspectives that include our neighborhoods but do not get stuck there?

When communities of faith do broaden their views, they sometimes respond to their immediate neighborhoods with little awareness of how narrow and parochial many of these areas are— in the United States, neighborhoods are commonly structured according to racial identity and class status. Traveling can help us broaden our horizons in important ways that are transformative not only for the world but for the church itself.

Still, there are some roadblocks. One of these is that traveling is still often seen as something exotic, something that's not part of the heart of the Christian life. Short-term mission trips, for instance, which are becoming increasingly popular in congregations that can afford to fund them, tend to be seen as interesting diversions in the life of a community of faith. Unfortunately, they are rarely allowed to shape the basic identity of these communities, and they are hardly ever considered relevant when it comes to belief and faith.

These are the problems the present book aims to remedy. Perhaps the most surprising insight presented here is that traveling is so deeply rooted in our traditions that many of them fail to make sense without it. Consider again how much of the material of the Jewish and Christian traditions actually developed on the road. There is nothing static about Abraham, regarded as one of the pillars of the faith. He developed his relationship with God when sent by God on a strange journey with his clan, far away from home.

The people of Israel spent a good amount of time on the road. Their stories speak of slavery in the lands of a foreign empire called Egypt, of an exodus from Egypt and of forty years of wandering in the wilderness. On this journey they learned important theological lessons, not all of them easy or pleasant. These lessons included a deepening of their understanding of God as well as profound challenges to outdated images portraying God as defender of the dominant power. Clearly God was not the God of the empire but the God of the people.

Later, the Jewish people were exiled to Babylon, the heart of another empire. In this exile they developed a new set of fresh and earth-shattering theological insights. Many of the biblical materials on creation, for instance, were produced during this exile as the people began to understand that their God was not subject to the empire that enslaved them but the creator of a world that allowed for alternatives—a place where even widows, orphans and strangers could flourish.

In the New Testament, Jesus' ministry takes place almost entirely on the road; he is a person who has "nowhere to lay his head" (Lk 9:58). Travel provides the setting of Jesus' birth when his family finds itself on the road by Roman decree and there is no room in the inn. Jesus' subsequent travels include migration as a child refugee to Egypt, ministerial journeys to remote areas of Galilee and budding economic centers around the Sea of Galilee, journeys along the border and into the borderlands, and a journey to metro-

politan Jerusalem. The Gospel of Luke adds a visit to Jerusalem as
a child, and the Gospel of John speaks of several journeys to this
metropolis. Following Jesus often meant traveling with him, and
the number of those who traveled was not limited to the twelve
disciples whom we recognize by name. Among those on the road
with Jesus were men and women from all walks of life.

The apostle Paul was locationally challenged in his own way, cov-
ering much larger distances than Jesus. On his travels Paul established churches in various parts of the Roman Empire, often in
situations of great pressure and tension, which he describes this
way: "Three times I was shipwrecked; for a night and a day I was
adrift at sea; on frequent journeys, in danger from rivers, dangers
from bandits, danger from my own people, danger from Gentiles,
danger in the city, danger in the wilderness, danger at sea, danger
from false brothers and sisters; in toil and hardship, through many
a sleepless night, hungry and thirsty, often without food, cold and
naked" (2 Cor 11:25-27). The book of Acts, which describes many of
Paul's travels, for good reasons calls Christians the people of "the
Way" (Acts 9:2; 19:9, 23; 22:4; 24:14, 22).

Perhaps one of the most important theological challenges travel
poses to the Christian life is summarized in the letter to the Hebrews: "Here we have no lasting city, but we are looking for the city
that is to come" (Heb 13:14). Christianity is what takes place on the
road. Travel, it appears therefore, is more than a metaphor of the
Christian faith. Location and constant relocation are central
matters of the Christian life.

Traveling is thus a central topic for faith and life from beginning
to end. But traveling is not just one thing. It comes in many forms
and shapes, and not everyone needs to travel as extensively as others.
Nevertheless, those who travel are in a position to make important
contributions in today's world. These include a habit of thinking on
one's feet, the broadening of horizons, a flexibility that comes with

having to give up control, various challenges to the status quo and a much-needed awareness of our own limits and finitude.

Travelers who spend time on the road experience in their very being what is at the heart of the Jewish-Christian traditions and what took philosophers thousands of years to understand: a new appreciation for small, particular experiences of life, out of which broader universal ideas grow. Theology and philosophy born on the road differ fundamentally from theology and philosophy based on big concepts and ideas proposed by dominant powers.

Finally, those who find themselves on the road without safety nets often develop special bonds and relationships with other people. One year, when my wife and I were traveling off the beaten path in the heart of Baja California, Mexico, with our young children for a few days, we met a young couple in a Unimog, an old German off-road military vehicle that happened to have been built the year I was born. Traveling together for a while not only made sense due to the remoteness of the area but also led to deep conversations and encounters that would not have otherwise taken place. This experience of vagabonding helped us to imagine how much more migrants must experience special bonds and relationships on their journeys, traveling without vehicles, with little water and in constant danger of being detected and deported.

No travel ever occurs in a vacuum. Travelers' individual experiences are framed by larger structures, which the travelers themselves may never realize. Power, as well as the lack of power, plays an important role in our travels. Becoming aware of these things is part of the broadening of our horizons, so let us explore where our journeys take us.

one

The Judeo-Christian Traditions on the Road

Theological Reflections on Travel

Don't trust a thought discovered
while sitting in your chair.

FRIEDRICH NIETZSCHE

WE OFTEN GRASP MORE ABOUT GOD on a walk than through a book."[1] Thus begins theologian Frederick Herzog's book *God-Walk*. Although many of our contemporary churches are oblivious to it, this wisdom reverberates throughout the Judeo-Christian traditions. If all the stories that deal with traveling, walking and journeying were taken out of the Bible, there would not be a whole lot left. Even the apostle Paul, celebrated by some as the greatest theologian of all time, developed his thoughts on the road.

Journeys and walks are central to the Christian life, and if we ignore this we will pay a price. Herzog took walks seriously. He often would meet with his students while walking on the grounds of Duke University or through his neighborhood in Durham, North Carolina, which bordered on low-income apartments. He preferred to walk from his house to the university and back, and whenever a student tried to offer him a ride, he responded, "I don't believe in that." In his office, Herzog did not have pictures of his great theological teachers in Europe and the United States but of William Edwards, an African American sharecropper and fireman, later a paraplegic, from whom he learned what he called the "Bible-in-hand method."

To make sense, Herzog believed, the Bible had to be read out in the fields where people worked, on the journey of life and in the midst of the struggle. One of the lessons he learned from the Civil Rights struggle was that thinking always had to be done on one's feet; none of his teachers had clued him in to that and this insight is still missing from much of our teaching today. One of Herzog's favorite stanzas from the great African American liberation hymns was "Stony the road we trod, bitter the chastening rod, felt in the day when hope unborn had died." It is no accident that Herzog quoted this in the last piece he wrote before his death.[2]

The Bible-in-hand method is closely related to what Herzog often called "the street Jesus": "The Jesus of the road is key today because he teaches us limits of human control within which alone the engine of historical change can move history on construc-tively."[3] It is true: Jesus spent more time on the road than sitting in church. The challenge that emerges from these journeys is not just a practical one but one that cuts to the heart of our faith. The identity of the divine itself is at stake: "We cannot help discovering God's character in a new way, since walking together with Jesus gets us in conflict over who God is."[4] God looks different from the dusty roads of Galilee than from the safety of the temple in Jerusalem. Today, God looks different from the street level of our cities than from the corner offices of economic, political and religious priv-ilege. Walking with Jesus is no trivial matter, as the disciples inevi-tably discovered, and the challenge continues today.

The basic document of the Christian traditions, the Bible, is not a static book that lends itself to a sedentary lifestyle or to a religion of inert privilege. Just the opposite: the Bible is a dynamic collection of a great variety of books, many written on journeys, in the midst of nomadic wanderings, during exiles and through the kinds of open-ended tensions and struggles with which many travelers are familiar. The Bible is fairly unique among the writings of classical world literature in that its texts were not produced predominantly by those holding privilege and might; in the Bible common people and their concerns have a voice. As such, the Bible prefigures a major shift in the understanding of world literature, which postcolonial theorist Homi Bhabha describes in the following way: "Where, once, the transmission of national traditions was the major theme of a world literature, perhaps we can now suggest that transnational histories of migrants, the colonized, or political refugees . . . may be the terrains of world literature."[5] Unfortunately, much of Christianity today seems to have forgotten—or perhaps even repressed—this shift from the center to the margins. The good news is that there are more and more voices today reclaiming this heritage.

In the Bible we hear stories of migrants (beginning with Abraham himself, who leaves home being promised a better life), the colonized (the people of Israel at various states in their history under pressure from the surrounding empires, including Jewish people in New Testament times) and political refugees (including Jesus' own family when he was a child). In addition, there are stories of messengers and prophets who are put on the road by God to unsettle and disrupt the privileged who are living sedentary lives. There is something about these stories that is not only deeply challenging to those who are used to resting comfortably but also deeply encouraging for the majority of humanity who do not enjoy this luxury.

Old Testament Journeys

The Hebrew Bible—what Christians call the Old Testament—cannot be imagined without travel stories, as travel is deeply interwoven with its messages. The story of Israel begins with an emigrant named Abraham, revered by Jews, Muslims and Christians alike. The travels of Abraham and his clan are much more interesting and complex than is commonly assumed. The big step that Abraham took, leaving his home and family, is well known, but the ancient stories do not tell us much about it. All we are told is that Abraham follows God's call: "Go from your country and your kindred and your father's house to the land that I will show you. I will make of you a great nation, and I will bless you, and make your name great, so that you will be a blessing" (Gen 12:1-2). No matter how triumphalistic the end of this journey seems and how high the hopes of the travelers may have been, every migrant who has been in a similar situation knows how painful it is to leave home, family and friends.

The Abraham story contains other stories that make clear the tensions and hardships of the journey. Immediately after arriving in Canaan, Abraham and his clan are forced to migrate to Egypt, and he is compelled to "reside there as an alien," like every other migrant in history, because of a famine. In Egypt Abraham's wife, Sarah, is "taken into Pharaoh's house" and is forced to become his concubine because Abraham, aware of his precarious situation, is afraid to identify her as his wife (Gen 12:10-20). This story too resembles the stories of migrant travelers throughout history and today, showing the lack of power of those who migrate, and it reminds us of the fact that migrant women's experiences of travel are usually even more troubled than those of men; they are often the lowest of the low. The account of Abraham and Sarah traveling to Egypt is another travel story that broadens our horizons and teaches us something about God and ourselves, as God does not hesitate to take the side of the migrant travelers and bails them out.

The Abraham stories also include the tragic travel narrative of Hagar, a slave woman who at some point was the maid of Sarah, and of Ishmael, the son of Abraham and Hagar. Hagar and Ishmael are sent into the desert by Abraham soon after the birth of Isaac, Abraham's son with Sarah. The two share the fate of many refugees, not traveling voluntarily but being displaced by the powers that be and having no place to go. Eventually they run out of water. This is the plight these days of many migrants from southern Mexico and Central America who have never experienced the barrenness of the desert and die in the Arizona desert after crossing the border into the United States.

To be sure, broadened theological horizons alone are not going to help in such a desperate situation. Something else is needed. In the story we are told that "God opened [Hagar's] eyes and she saw a well of water" (Gen 21:19). The text draws the theological conclusion that "God was with the boy, and he grew up" (Gen 21:20). Some of the existential challenges of travelers who are not in control, and whose survival therefore depends solely on God, are reflected in the notion of the "wilderness experience," coined by womanist theologian Delores Williams and modeled after the experience of Hagar and Ishmael in the desert.[6] For Williams, such a wilderness experience is the fundamental experience of African American women in the United States who are forced to make a way where there is no way. This experience of not being in control, related to the need for guidance from others and help from God, remains one of the fundamental experiences of all travelers, albeit to various degrees.

Travel is so deeply interwoven with the messages of the Old Testament that even what some consider the "creeds" distilled in these writings are shaped by travel. Such Old Testament creeds differ fundamentally from the rather static creeds developed by Christianity centuries after Jesus when it became the official religion of the Roman Empire, beginning with the Nicene Creed in 325 CE. To be sure, even the Nicene Creed becomes a whole lot more dynamic when seen in the light of these ancient creeds, as I have argued elsewhere.[7]

Instead of using conceptual language and giving metaphysical definitions, the creeds of the Old Testament tell stories, and they deal with experiences of God on the road:

> A wandering Aramean was my ancestor; he went down into Egypt and lived there as an alien, few in number, and there he became a great nation, mighty and populous. When the Egyptians treated us harshly and afflicted us, by imposing hard labor on us, we cried to the LORD, the God of our ancestors; the LORD heard our voice and saw our affliction, our toil, and our oppression. The LORD brought us out of Egypt with a mighty hand and an outstretched arm, with a terrifying display of power, and with signs and wonders; and he brought us into this place and gave us this land, a land flowing with milk and honey. (Deut 26:5-9)

Confessions like these are at the very heart of the biblical traditions, and they are designed to remind those who think they have arrived in any sort of "promised land" about the conflictual journeys of the past. In light of these confessions, the conflictual stories of the present are bound to appear in new light.

We can leave the details to biblical scholarship, whether the Aramean referred to was a nomad or a fugitive, and to whom this reference applies. What matters is that this Aramean ancestor was a wanderer in conflictual times and that today this biblical passage is still part of the Jewish Seder, the ritual celebration at the beginning of Passover. Thus, the importance of this story about the wandering Aramean for the Jewish and Christian traditions can hardly be overestimated. Already the initial story mentioned in the passage, the travel of the Aramean ancestor to Egypt, is full of tensions. Joseph is sold into slavery by his brothers and taken to Egypt, where he is bought by one of the Pharaoh's officials (Gen 37:12-36). As Joseph goes from rags to riches in Egypt, making a fortune by selling grain to the Egyptians during a severe famine, Joseph's brothers are forced to migrate to Egypt in order to buy grain (Gen 41:53–42:5); it is away from home in Egypt that they finally reconcile. Yet although God promises support for the Aramean tribe when Joseph's brothers and his father, Jacob, eventually move to Egypt (Gen 46:1-4), the Israelites are going to be enslaved there. This creates the need for another major journey.

What does all of this mean for us as people of faith in the twenty-first century? One of the major lessons of these experiences on the road is that there can never be any detached and neutral theology that stays safely on the sidelines of life. People of faith never find themselves in a vacuum or on neutral ground; they are always on a journey. If they forget this, they betray their heritage. Neutrality is never an option for theologians. This will become clearer as we get deeper into theology done on the road.

The travels of Moses help us further understand who God is and who God's people are called to be. Early in his life Moses escapes the Pharaoh's orders that all young Hebrew boys be killed, only to be subsequently adopted by Pharaoh's daughter and raised as an Egyptian prince. Princes do not associate with common people, and Moses might have ended his life in the safety and comfort of the court if not for an encounter with some of the enslaved Hebrews that wakes him out of his royal slumbers and puts him on the road. When he observes how Hebrew slaves are being abused, Moses overreacts and kills one of the slave masters in anger and has to flee the country. It is only later, when Moses is a political refugee who has worked for a considerable time in the land of Midian raising a family, that God speaks to him. God's speech—out of a burning bush that is not consumed by fire, as the story goes—prepares him for another journey. Based on the relationship to the traveling fathers—God is "the God of Abraham, the God of Isaac, and the God of Jacob" (Ex 3:6)—God tells Moses:

> I have observed the misery of my people who are in Egypt; I have heard their cry on account of their taskmasters. Indeed, I know their sufferings, and I have come down to deliver them from the Egyptians, and to bring them out of that land to a good and broad land, a land flowing with milk and honey, to the country of the Canaanites, the Hittites, the Amorites, the Perizzites, the Hivites, and the Jebusites. The cry of the Israelites has now come to me; I have also seen how the Egyptians oppress them. So come, I will send you to Pharaoh to bring my people, the Israelites, out of Egypt. (Ex 3:7-10)

Unfortunately, because people have been so mesmerized by the miracle of the burning bush, the content of the speech has often been neglected. One thing, however, is clear at this point: in the midst of travels past, present and future, the people develop a substantially broadened understanding of God. Moses is no exception here, as his image of God must have been turned from its head to its feet, from the God of the rulers to the God of the slaves.

The image of God as liberator from oppression, blatantly taking the side of the oppressed against the oppressors and leading the Israelites on an enormous "walkout," as it were, is a powerful one. It is so challenging that theologians and people of faith have tried to contain it ever since. Some choose to speculate on the meaning of the mysterious announcement of the name of God as "I AM WHO I AM" or "I WILL BE WHO I WILL BE" (Ex 3:14) without bothering to look back to the particular journey on which this God leads his people. Others focus on the miraculous qualities of a bush going up in flames without being consumed, or on abstract notions of divine revelation, without much concern for what actually is being revealed. Others worry that the liberation of the Israelites is leading straight into another conquest, this time of the Canaanites.

We must not romanticize the liberation of slaves from bondage to an empire. The Exodus traditions themselves mention a decades-long and arduous journey to the Promised Land beset by failures, sufferings, hardships, setbacks and repeated struggles. Even the liberated slaves get tired and begin to fantasize about the proverbial "fleshpots" of Egypt (Ex 16:3). Nevertheless, God continues to be on the road with his people, struggling with them, never giving up on them. And while these slaves' fantasies suggest that they crave another empire, some of the biblical traditions have a different story to tell.

The Hebrew slaves' drawn-out wandering to the Promised Land most likely did not lead to an empire-style conquest. What little data we have points to the possibility that they joined forces with other Hebrews who already resided in the land—"Hebrew" meaning "social outcast" or "troublemaker." Many of these Hebrews of the land were loosely connected farmers. When they were joined by the more recent arrivals from Egypt via the desert, they rose up against the kings of the powerful cities of Canaan, struggling for the liberation of the rural population and other misfits.[8] These travel stories resemble contemporary migration stories in which travel is above all a matter of survival, creating new opportunities for life when it goes well. As with all travel under pressure, these travel experiences broaden people's horizons.

While travel is thus a constant theme in the Hebrew Bible, its authors also warn against a lack of movement and a tendency to rest comfortably. "Those who lie on beds of ivory, and lounge on their couches" (Amos 6:4) are missing what is going on in the world and become part of the problem. The prophet Amos suggests a connection between the elites who build "houses of hewn stone" and plant "pleasant vineyards" and the exploitation of the poor (Amos 5:11). The remedy for this is not charity for the poor or services of worship but the establishment of justice: "Take away from me the noise of your songs," God says. "I will not listen to the melody of your harps. But let justice roll down like waters, and righteousness like an ever-flowing stream" (Amos 5:23-24). The God who moves toward justice invites the people to join in this movement: "Seek me and live" (Amos 5:4).

It should be clear by now that travels in the Hebrew Bible are not undertaken for the sake of entertainment and tourism. Travel is tied to tension and displacement. It is also the context in which new hope and new encounters with God develop. In the sixth century BCE, the leaders of Judah and many of the people are forced to travel again—this time into exile in Babylonia. While the people have long understood God as the God traveling with them to particular locations, at this juncture they begin to understand God as God of the whole world. While the people have understood that God was on the road with them, they now begin to realize that God is even greater.

The Judeo-Christian doctrine of creation has its origins in these experiences of a greater God: the God whom the people of Judah and Israel worship can no longer be envisioned merely as a local or tribal deity. This God is now seen as the creator of the whole world, who is at work in the whole world, greater than even the Babylonian Empire. This faith in the creator is not a triumphalistic vision of yet another empire but a vision that encourages the endurance and resistance of the people in exile and keeps alive their hope for an eventual return.

An understanding that God is at work not just in particular faith communities but also in the world at large could make a tremendous difference in our churches today. It would break open the narcissism that so often keeps us tied not only to our church buildings and pews, but also to our own ideas and our own ways of life. Such churches, even if they seem to flourish for a time, are ultimately doomed because they miss the God who is on the move in the world. Adding a little outreach is not enough either, as self-centered churches that engage in outreach ministries often assume their task is to take a God who is primarily housed in their sanctuaries out into the world. What these churches miss is the opportunity to meet God at work in the world and in creation. Not only is the God of self-centered and static faith communities too narrow; the one who is worshiped in such settings may be someone other than the God of Moses, Abraham and the people of Israel.

Of course, not just any old vision of God at work outside the church will do. If it is not clear that God is at work in particular ways, tied to particular stories and engaged in particular purposes and journeys, God will quickly be identified with the gods of the empire. This happens more often than we realize, not only in the past but also today. During the Babylonian exile, the temptation was to identify the God of Moses and Abraham with the god of the empire. Today, the temptation is to identify this God with the god of money and dominant power.

It is crucial, therefore, to hold together two things: God remains at work in a world in which many people find themselves in situations of exile, and this particular God is greater than all the gods of the empires of the world combined. Putting together these two insights leads us to search for the particular places where God is at work, or where God continues to move, in the midst of the pressures and complications of enslavement and exile.

New Testament Journeys

In the New Testament, many of the major experiences of God are also located on the road. Jesus' disciples get to know him while traveling with him through remote provinces, distant borderlands, small villages and eventually the capital city Jerusalem. Paul meets an apparition of Jesus while traveling and spends the rest of his life traveling the roads of the Roman Empire.

Jesus' ministry takes place almost entirely on the road. While he is identified as a person from Galilee—the place where he grew up, which was far from the centers of power of the day—he refuses to take up permanent residence: "Foxes have holes, and birds of the air have nests; but the Son of Man has nowhere to lay his head" (Lk 9:58). Jesus' birth takes place on the road, on a journey to Bethlehem that was ordered by imperial interests. Having nowhere to lay his head, Jesus' mother "laid him in a manger, because there was no place for them in the inn" (Lk 2:7). Presumably they did not stay long. Jesus' childhood also included traumatic migratory travel to Egypt and life as a political refugee (Mt 2:13-15). None of these travels was voluntary or for pleasure. The first was on account of a Roman census for tax purposes. The second was forced by Herod, a vassal of the Roman emperor, who had all children under the age of two killed in order to get rid of even the slightest challenge to his power.

Our horizons are broadened by these early travels in Jesus' life in a rather uncomfortable way. God appears to travel not in the center but on the margins of the Roman Empire—an empire that considered itself divinely ordained. Still more, God appears to travel against the grain of this empire and to threaten it. Deep theological questions emerge here that should not be ignored: Why is Christ born on the road, in a manger in a stable, in the company of cattle and day laborers who herd other people's sheep? Why does God travel with a refugee family in Egypt rather than with Herod, the lawfully appointed ruler of the land?

These questions do not get resolved and put to rest as Jesus continues his ministry. Even the people who accompany Jesus on the road, including his closest circle of supporters, are puzzled and confused. What do we make of the fact that after spending an extended amount of time traveling with Jesus, his disciples still have difficulty understanding what he's doing?

This confusion and lack of understanding show how deep-seated our static views of God, the world and dominant power really are. The persona of Simon Peter in the Gospel of Mark is perhaps the most telling, as he has tremendous difficulties letting go of his own static images of God and divine power. When Jesus proclaims that "the Son of Man must undergo great suffering, and be rejected by the elders, the chief priests, and the scribes, and be killed, and after three days rise again," Peter takes him aside and rebukes him (Mk 8:31-32). When Jesus is transfigured on a mountain and Elijah and Moses appear to him, Peter wants to end the journey right there and then and build dwellings in the place (Mk 9:2-8). Peter's final denial of Jesus in Jerusalem after Jesus is captured is probably one of the best-known details of the Gospels (Mk 14:66-72, with parallels in all four Gospels): it was dangerous to be identified with Jesus' travels at the margins of empire.

On another journey to Capernaum, a center of commerce by the Sea of Galilee, the disciples argue about who is the greatest. Jesus' answer is well-known and stands in direct contradiction to the logic of static power: "Whoever wants to be first must be last of all and servant of all" (Mk 9:35). The lessons on the road have to do with experiences of powerful alternatives to the status quo. In Jesus, God is experienced not as static but as on the move with the "least of these" and those who hear Jesus' consistent call: "Follow me."

Perhaps nowhere is this more painfully clear than when Jesus' family comes to visit him. While the conservative status quo then and now wants us to believe that family bonds are supremely binding and ultimate, Jesus holds an entirely different view. Pointing to his companions on the journey rather than to the ones who represent home, he states, "Here are my mother and my brothers! Whoever does the will of God is my brother and sister and mother" (Mk 3:31-35). While Jesus' definition of family does not exclude families of origin by default, in this episode on the road he completely changes our view of what matters. This new perspective can be gained only on the road, when people are ready to leave home, family and friends and embark on a journey following Jesus.

The one who wants to bury his father before embarking on the journey is confronted harshly by Jesus: "Let the dead bury their own dead; but as for you, go and proclaim the kingdom of God." And the one who—quite understandably—wants to say goodbye to his kin, Jesus reprimands: "No one who puts a hand to the plow and looks back is fit for the kingdom of God" (Lk 9:59-62). Jesus seems to be deeply concerned that the static places of home and family will end up holding us back. After he returns home at one point early in his ministry, his own family feels that he has gone too far and they turn against him, making efforts to restrain him. His own family seems to agree with those who said, "He has gone out of his mind" (Mk 3:20-21). This statement must have appeared so disrespectful to ancient ears that only Mark reports it.

Many of those who spent time traveling with Jesus were working people, and traveling imposed considerable burdens on them. Peter states it bluntly: "Look, we have left everything and followed you." Jesus' response concludes with the well-known but still challenging phrase that "many who are first will be last, and the last will be first," noting that those who have left home and family to travel with him will receive many other "houses, brothers and sisters, mothers and children, and fields, with persecutions" as well as eternal life (Mk 10:28-31). Apparently the new community that is organized on the road has its own rewards, despite the hardships associated with leading an antiestablishment life. While we have no evidence that the Jesus movement was very large in its day, it was clearly diverse. In addition to the twelve disciples, the traveling movement included men and women from various segments of society—even a group of wealthy women who supported Jesus' work. Among these was the wife of one of Herod's officials (Lk 8:2-3), which is a testimony to the power of the movement to change the lives of even the most privileged. We might read this as an encouraging sign that the journey of a camel through the eye of the needle, while impossible for humans (as the disciples astutely note), is indeed possible with the help of God (Mk 10:23-27).

The lessons of travel are not always clear in the midst of the journey. Sometimes we understand only later, after we return home. This is the case in the Emmaus story, which is unique to the Gospel of Luke. Walking together with the resurrected Christ to a village near Jerusalem, two disciples recognize him only after they arrive and invite him into their house. Only in hindsight are their eyes opened: "Were not our hearts burning within us while he was taking to us on the road, while he was opening the scriptures to us?" (Lk 24:32). It seems that the most important part of any journey is this experience of having one's eyes opened, of returning home and beginning to see things in a new light. The theological question raised by the Emmaus story is this: How is the resurrected Christ traveling with all of us when we are on the road in our time? How might traveling with this unrecognized Christ help us see things in a new light when we return home?

Interpreting the Gospel of John, African biblical scholar Musa Dube and Seattle-based biblical scholar Jeffrey Staley note, "The biblical story is at times a travel narrative; it commands its readers to travel. Consequently, the privileging of one historical [period (i.e., ancient times)] in determining its meaning is ideologically suspect."[9] The travels of Jesus and his fellow travelers are not merely a matter of the past; in a very important sense they are still taking place. Those who seek to find meaning in these ancient travel stories today need to travel as well and consider the stories' impact on their current location. In the words of Dube and Staley, "The journey we choose to participate in, and the space we choose to inhabit in our reading practices are, therefore, acts that have an impact on our worlds and our neighbors' worlds."[10] In other words, travel makes a difference, but we have to choose wisely.

As travel opens our eyes to the tensions of this world, we are forced to choose sides. Dube and Staley conclude, commenting on the Gospel of John, "The Johannine narrative is best seen as a site of struggle for power amongst different parties. And we, as readers, cannot be neutral in this struggle."[11] Clearly, not just any travel will do. As we see God at work in the travel of migrants, refugees and exiles, those of us who have the privilege to travel under less pressure have a choice to make. Do we continue to travel with the privileged elites and make every effort not to be bothered? Or do we travel in ways that allow us to stay connected with the common people?

For Christians, that decision depends on where we see Jesus on the road. Herzog would raise a deceptively simple question: What is Jesus doing now?[12] This brings the familiar question "What would Jesus do?" closer to home. Let's take stock: Where and with whom do we see Christ traveling on today's roads, and how might that influence our own travels?

During his travels Jesus encountered many people, including women and minorities, to whom the religious leaders of the day had little connection. On one journey described in the Gospel of John, Jesus travels from Judea to Galilee, passing through Samaria, where he encounters a local woman. Although the disciples can barely conceal their misgivings about the fact that Jesus is talking to a foreign woman of different ethnicity and religion (Jn 4:27), this woman becomes one of the preachers of the good news to her people (Jn 4:1-42). Another woman on the road, a Gentile of Syrophoenician origin, manages to do what none of the disciples could have accomplished: she changes Jesus' mind about foreigners. Jesus, who up to that point had believed himself to be sent to Israel only, is effectively persuaded by this woman to extend his ministry and heal her daughter (Mk 7:24-30). Amazingly, the horizon that is broadened here is not just the human one but the divine: through Jesus, the divine mission itself begins to travel further. Without Jesus' travels to Samaria and the region of Tyre, none of these things would have happened. Travel thus becomes a foundational aspect of the evolving mission of Christianity.

Back in that day, the only way to truly encounter Jesus was to be on the road. Merely sitting or standing in worship services would not have equipped people to grasp what he was about. Not surprisingly, he got kicked out of one synagogue where people were unable to see the bigger picture (Lk 4:16-30).

The apostle Paul seems to have understood this need to be on the road as well. He covered even larger distances than Jesus and established churches in various parts of the Roman Empire, including in its very center in Rome. While Paul's travels are certainly not the travels of a tourist, neither are they the routine travels of a prominent businessperson. The New Testament is full of the challenges he experienced along the way (see 2 Cor 11:25-27), many of which involved time spent in the empire's prisons. Clearly, travelers who pose a challenge to the powers that be will find themselves challenged.

Those who traveled the roads of the Roman Empire were expected to conform to the empire's rules. That Paul found himself in and out of Roman prisons on his journeys was hardly due to harmless misunderstandings; his message led him there directly. How could the empire afford to let someone off the hook who preached "a stumbling block to Jews and foolishness to Gentiles," a God whose "foolishness is wiser than human wisdom" and whose "weakness is stronger than human strength" (1 Cor 1:23, 25)? What would pointing out the "rulers of this age, who are doomed to perish" (1 Cor 2:6) do to someone who traveled the roads built by these rulers? What would it mean for us today to travel like Paul, in a way that challenges the powers and principalities of our own age?

This is not merely a story about Paul; it is also a story about God. Paul is convinced that God is walking these roads with him, refusing to give in to the status quo. After all, this is the God who "chose what is low and despised in the world, things that are not, to reduce to nothing things that are" (1 Cor 1:28). The disagreement between Paul and the Roman Empire is not whether God exists but who God is. In the contemporary United States, we are faced with a similar question.

In the struggle against that which restricts us—the various forms of oppression and their manifestations we encounter on the road—we find freedom by siding with the true God against the false gods and by walking with Christ. On this journey we cannot avoid danger but we can confront and resist it: "For freedom Christ has set us free. Stand firm, therefore, and do not submit again to a yoke of slavery" (Gal 5:1).

For good reason the book of Acts, which is composed of travel stories, calls Christians the people of "the Way" (Acts 9:2; 19:9, 23; 22:4; 24:14, 22). The basic theological insights of the early church develop on the road. When the apostles Peter and John encounter a beggar lying at the gate of the temple in Jerusalem, they help him back on his feet and prepare him for the road. In Peter's words, "I have no silver or gold, but what I have I give you; in the name of Jesus Christ of Nazareth, stand up and walk" (Acts 3:6). Perhaps this account is less a gloss about disability and more an illustration of the effects of the good news in mobilizing people to join the walk of Christ in whatever way possible.

Christ himself was known to encourage people to "stand up and walk" (Mt 9:5). This encouragement to rise and walk contains various levels of meaning, including the ideas of "rising to the occasion," "rising up against what keeps us down," "uprising" and "rising with Christ." Appropriately, Herzog's family chose the motto "rise and walk" for his tombstone, and it would be fitting for all of us who seek to follow Christ who push against the static rules of our time that seek to keep us down. As people of the Way, Christians are put on a journey that is life-changing. It is on this journey that we encounter God, as Saul encounters Jesus on the road to Damascus (Acts 9:1-19). The result is that lives are changed—Saul becomes Paul—and that the world will never be the same.

If the earliest understandings of Jesus thus evolved on the road, it makes sense to talk about a *christologia viatorum* (a Christology of travelers and pilgrims) or a *christologia viae* (a Christology of the road).[13] Theologian Jürgen Moltmann has formulated the challenge in this way: "I am trying to think of Christ no longer statically, as one person in two natures or as historical personality. I am trying to grasp him dynamically, in the forward movement of God's history with the world."[14] Without following the movement of God in Christ we may miss the truth of our faith altogether.

Not only are dynamic visions of Christ more interesting and inspiring than static images; we desperately need these dynamic visions to draw us out of our static ways of thinking tied to static ways of being Christians. Everything comes to a halt when Christians sitting in church cannot think of other images of Christ than sitting at the right hand of God, waiting for the blow of the trumpet on judgment day. Images of a static eternity—often envisioned as a never-ending worship service with never-ending playing of harps and never-ending sitting, standing or kneeling—do not help us capture dynamic visions of Christ either.

None of these static conceptualizations relate to a Christ who is encountered on the road. Even otherwise difficult-to-understand doctrines like the two natures of Christ, one human and one divine, come alive and begin to make sense in the context of Jesus' life on the road. Christ's humanity and divinity are not abstract principles. Instead, what is human and what is divine are seen in how Jesus lives his life, which fills these categories with new meaning. God and humanity moving together in Jesus among the "least of these" surpasses our wildest imaginations.[15] Christianity comes alive only on the road.

Not only does static, nontraveling Christianity lack the dynamic of movement and action; it also gets stuck with the status quo. When the theologians of the church's Fourth Ecumenical Council in Chalcedon, 451 CE, asserted the dual nature of Christ as human and divine, they confirmed static images of humanity and divinity without realizing what they were doing. Divinity, in the dominant theologies of the day, was shaped by Greek concepts of immutability and impassibility, rendering Christ static and immobile. This problem could have been resolved by pointing to Jesus' life and ministry, making it clear that Jesus embodied new images of humanity and divinity on the road that were fundamentally different.

Images of God as resting on a throne at the top of the world, or as first unmoved mover (Aristotle), are for the most part images of dominant power. Such dominant power can be declared truly all-powerful only if nothing can ever influence or move it. According to this school of philosophy, if something is able to influence God, God is no longer omnipotent. This sort of power contrasts with what we know about the life and ministry of Jesus on the road. Jesus' actions do not reflect absolute power, and neither do the images of God on the road found in the Hebrew Bible, as discussed earlier in this chapter. If God's power were merely a one-way street, any effort to interact with God would be futile; not even prayer would make much sense.

A TRAVELING GOD, A JOURNEY OF FAITH

In all these stories, from the Hebrew Bible to the New Testament, God travels. Such a traveling God will never make sense to those who cling to the static top-down power of the empires of this world and their status quo religions, which constantly seek to shape Jewish and Christian faith. The Romans, for instance, knew what they were saying when they called the early Christians who would not conform to its rules "atheists." And they were right, from the perspective of status quo religion: a God who is on the road does not match the sort of theism that wants to see God at the top in the universe, unmoved and perfect.

Let us not forget, however, that in this ancient world, Christianity eventually found its place when it adapted to the expectations of the empire. Even the theological claim that Jesus was Son of God did not pose an insurmountable philosophical problem for the Romans; the imperial Jesus found himself in good company, as emperors were also considered sons of God. The problem that the empire could not resolve, however, had to do with the claim that this particular person, the anti-imperial Jesus of the road, was declared Son of God. A Son of God who traveled with the common people and did not obey the rules of the road imposed by the dominant powers, whether Jewish or Roman, could create only trouble for the empire.

One of the theological challenges that travel poses to the Christian life, as summarized in the letter to the Hebrews, is that "here we have no lasting city, but we are looking for the city that is to come" (Heb 13:14). Travel, it appears therefore, is more than just a metaphor of the Christian faith. Location and relocation are central matters in the Jewish-Christian traditions. Implied here is a critique of home and any of the other places where we may find ourselves. Ultimately, there is no place that can offer us a lasting home here and now, because home is often a place where the powers that be exert control most successfully. It is for this reason that Christians remain on the move. This is also the reason that Christians are to welcome others who are on the road: "Do not neglect to show hospitality to strangers" (Heb 13:2). Is it an accident that we hear in this verse a reference to Matthew 25:35: "I was a stranger and you welcomed me"?

Even Jerusalem, the holy place for Judaism, Islam and Christianity, might best be understood in the context of movement and travel. The book of Revelation sees it "coming down out of heaven from God" (Rev 21:10). This new Jerusalem is the place where our travels lead us, a place where there is no longer even a need for a temple, because God is present in fullness. In the new Jerusalem, the gates will remain open so that people can travel in and out freely at all times (Rev 21:22-27). Migration will no longer be a crime, and travel will be unrestricted and encouraged.

These reflections on travel lead us to a deeper understanding of the nature of theology. Anyone who does theology on the road knows that theology is always contextual, always engaged, never neutral. Put a different way, only a theology that refuses to travel can uphold the illusion that neutrality exists, and only a sedentary theology will talk about God in abstract and universal terms. Unfortunately, such a theology deludes itself because all that is served by this sort of neutrality, abstraction and universalization is the status quo. And this status quo, not surprisingly, benefits from being static; it is how privilege is secured in the hands of a few.

What matters for a theology informed by life on the road are particulars rather than abstract universals. The question is not "Is there a God in general?" but "Where can God be found?" and "Where is God traveling and moving?" As we begin to pay attention in our theologies to the places where God is traveling, we might hear again the ancient invitation, "Follow me." This is the difference between asking the popular question "Is God on our side?" and asking the less-common question "Are we on God's side?" The former is usually answered in the affirmative by theologians of the status quo. The latter is much more interesting and cannot be answered with a universal affirmation, as it invites us on a journey with God, where constant movement and navigation are required.

The question of whether God is on our side allows us to stay put. Those who operate from this perspective create room for God in their buildings, where they imagine God dwells with them in comfort, or they imagine they have to carry God around with them when they travel. This has disastrous consequences for religious travel, as it precludes the possibility of searching for and finding God in other places, at work with different people and problems. We will come back to this in chapter four.

There is a strange connectedness among those who travel on similar journeys that those who stay put will never know. In the words of Herzog: "Walking the roads of the South [in the United States] I often thought that people walking for justice here were sometimes closer to other walkers all over the world than they were to sisters and brothers sitting in nearby precinct halls or church pews."[16] Ecumenical and interreligious efforts take on a completely different dynamic when people travel together: instead of sitting around tables comparing abstract and static theological ideas, those on common journeys engage in a deeper theological exchange, sharing and comparing actual experiences with the divine and with the theological images they encounter. Theology on the road knows that theory emerges from praxis rather than the other way around. This matter will be developed further in the following chapters.

In a world where more and more people are traveling—whether as migrants, refugees, pilgrims or tourists—we are now ready to reclaim the wisdom of our traditions, much of which has been lost. The experiences of migratory travelers especially can help us deepen our theological understanding of travel in the Judeo-Christian tradition. And it's not just our theology that changes; other ways of understanding are transformed as well, along with how we look at the world in general. As anthropologist Steven Vertovec has pointed out, "For a long time, many anthropologists' lack of interest in migration was due to their overriding concern with elucidating patterns of social and cultural order that underpinned societies, rather than with unraveling processes of change (which migration represents in many ways)."[17] As we move away from an obsession with social and cultural order, broader horizons open up that are bound to transform Christianity and communities of faith as well.

Anthropologist James Clifford summarizes what is at stake: "Theory is always written from some 'where,' and that 'where' is less a place than itineraries: different, concrete histories of dwelling, immigration, exile, migration."[18] Paradoxically, as anthropologists are beginning to realize, the hosts are sometimes more experienced in travel than their guests. A whole new way of looking at the world, at others and at ourselves emerges when we begin to think from the perspective of the road. Things will never be the same.

two

Travel, Tourism and Migration

Experiences on the Road

Travel is fatal to prejudice, bigotry and narrow-mindedness, and many of our people need it sorely on these accounts. Broad, wholesome, charitable views of men and things cannot be acquired by vegetating in one little corner of the earth all one's lifetime."[1] These famous words were written by none other than Mark Twain. Few of us would disagree: Is not travel about broadening one's horizons and learning new things? I still remember my family's travels through Europe, which did much to broaden my horizons as a child. We visited many places where previous generations of my family never had the opportunity to go. The only opportunity my grandfathers had to travel out of the country was when they were sent to war as soldiers in Germany's armies, one to France in World War I and the other to Russia in World War II.

What is often overlooked, however, is that broadening one's horizons requires work. It does not happen by default. Twain's comments are found in his travelogue *The Innocents Abroad*, which chronicles the failures of a group of travelers to push beyond prejudice and bigotry. For the most part, these failures have nothing to do with a lack of good intention on the part of the travelers. Things are more complex than that. Despite their best efforts, the travelers on a cruise through Europe and the Holy Land discover they do not care much about France, Italy and Spain.

Twain's humorous language is worth quoting: "We galloped through the Louvre, the Pitti, the Uffizi, the Vatican—all the galleries— and through the pictured and frescoed churches of Venice, Naples, and the cathedrals of Spain; some of us said that certain of the great works of the old masters were glorious creations of genius (we found it out in the guide-book, though we got hold of the wrong pictures sometimes) and the others said they were disgraceful old daubs."[2] Twain's descriptions reflect the tensions within the family of my childhood as well: some of us found the artifacts of high culture boring, while others made valiant efforts to understand and appreciate. Even when afforded the opportunity to travel, not everyone can muster an attitude of amazement and awe for very long. Besides, many of us are beset with a nagging reminder that the great cathedrals and castles we are supposed to admire were built by the forced labor of our ancestors. In my family, it was my mother who helped me understand some of these discrepancies— the guides for the most part never mentioned any of this.

The only place that finally gets Twain's group of tourists excited is the Holy Land. They feel strangely familiar with it, having been raised with the Bible:

> We fell into raptures by the barren shores of Galilee; we pon-
> dered at Tabor and at Nazareth; we exploded into poetry over
> the questionable loveliness of Esdraelon; we meditated at
> Jezreel and Samaria over the missionary zeal of Jehu; we
> rioted—fairly rioted among the holy places of Jerusalem; we
> bathed in Jordan and the Dead Sea, reckless whether our
> accident-insurance policies were extra-hazardous or not, and

brought away so many jugs of precious water from both places that all the country from Jericho to the mountains of Moab will suffer from drought this year.[3]

When I was growing up, none of the members of my immediate family had the opportunity to travel to the Holy Land, but we could not help but notice the kind of fetishism Twain describes. It seemed to have taken hold of many of our friends and relatives who made it there and back. I recall a number of stories about water from the Jordan River and bathing in the Dead Sea.

Twain's entertaining observations remind us of certain ways of relating to surroundings and to other people that not only are typical of certain types of tourism but also continue to pervade society in our own time. Even if we try to develop relationships, we find that our experiences of other people and other places, even the ones that seem raw and genuine, are filtered through the lenses of our preconceived ideas. Moreover, many of our ideas and beliefs are so deep-seated that they shape the way we relate to the world, often without our being aware of it.

After his group travels on from the Holy Land, according to Twain, nothing else interests the tourists—not even Egypt. Twain's experience demonstrates how religious beliefs travel with us and play a special role in shaping our relations to our environment and to other people. The disturbing truth is that such religious experiences shape us in ways that can be both detrimental and helpful.

Tourism's Complexities

Twain's nineteenth-century experiences with tourism were limited to an elite group of people who could afford it. Today, tourism is possible for millions of people who would otherwise never get to leave home. In contemporary Europe, tourism is nothing less than a way of life as people enjoy on average forty-two days of vacation from work each year. In the United States, where the average time off work is only thirteen days and where a whopping 33 percent check in with their employers during vacation, tourism is shaped by people trying to make use of what little time they have in the most effective ways.[4]

There are some benefits to tourism, even if the opportunities are limited. Having the opportunity to spend time on the road and away from the pressures of everyday work can support the broadening of horizons. In addition, it can also put everyday work in a different perspective and raise questions. I have fond memories of a month-long trip across the United States from North Carolina to California in the early 1990s in an old VW camper van, soon after my wife and I had moved to the United States from Germany. Driving an underpowered vehicle—this one had a fifty-horsepower diesel engine that was not powerful enough for an air conditioner; it was the kind I had driven as a student when I worked for the German postal service—forced us to take things slow. Going slow and keeping the windows open helped us get a sense not only of the vastness of the country but also of its real diversity and its tensions, which are often pushed under the rug by patriotic discourses. Finding out when crossing the state of Oklahoma that the Cherokee had not always been there, for instance, reminded us of the travels of others that were much slower and harder than ours—travels that were certainly not for pleasure.

Making the same journey across the country on a Greyhound bus would have taught us even more interesting lessons, to be sure, and there is some wisdom in traveling that way. Some people are convinced that there is no better way to get to know America than onboard a bus. At the same time, a trip by plane from North Carolina to California would have taught us considerably less about the country. For the past couple of years, making cross-country trips on a motorcycle to lectures and research sites has again put me close to many of the common people. Invariably, the bike is a conversation starter with all kinds of people, many of whom are eager to find out more about a lone traveler and to tell their own stories of the road.

In addition to all of this, traveling on a motorcycle also allows for more intimate encounters with the environment, its shapes and even its smells, its beauty but also its harshness. Thunderstorms and lightning, blinding dust storms in the desert, brutal heat waves in the South, freezing cold spells in the North, gusty winds on the Great Plains that can blow vehicles off the road, and endless geographical expanse inevitably leave their marks on the traveler who is exposed to them for extended periods of time. For me, camping out at night rather than staying in hotels further increases the intensity of the environment. Riding through populated areas adds other experiences, from being vulnerable to heavy traffic and road rage to being chased by dogs to receiving waves from children and others who dwell on the margins of society. Since I keep my vehicles in good shape, breakdowns and other mishaps are infrequent, but even those kinds of experiences add to the fascination of travel. Most people I have met in such situations genuinely care and are trying to help.

I do not always mention that I have traveled on a motorcycle when I arrive at my destination, especially when I lecture to more sheltered and privileged audiences. People tend to associate motorcycles not only with danger but also with all kinds of wild fantasies, and it would take a lecture in itself to explain. Nevertheless, the topics I talk about and that I research are invariably shaped by my experiences on the road, even when I do not mention them explicitly in my talks. My theology is definitely a theology of the road.

It is no secret that travel is closely related to matters of the economy, and tourism is no exception. For the most part, it is people with a certain economic privilege who can afford to travel for pleasure. People's economic standing also determines how far they can travel and at what levels of comfort. Those who have money can insulate themselves from the hardships of everyday life not only at home but also when traveling abroad. Even middle-class travelers recognize quickly that class differentials matter when traveling. Anyone who has spent much time traveling to other continents is aware of the considerable differences between business class and economy class on crowded overnight flights. Space in the economy class is reduced to the same degree that comfort and services are added in the higher classes, reflecting the growing divide between the one percent and everyone else. For those who can afford to stay at the top hotels of the world, there is little difference in comfort between São Paulo, Johannesburg, Shanghai, Frankfurt and New York. In these spaces of privilege, it is not even necessary to know a few words of another language. The words of a Hilton Hotels representative sum it up: "Each of our hotels is a little America."[5]

Tourism is a complex phenomenon, and it includes not only those who travel but also those who are visited. Increasingly, tourism is becoming a major aspect of economic production in various parts of the world, and whole regions depend on the income it generates. The tourism industry is constantly in flux as it parallels the global expansion of the economy, reaching further and further around the globe. Even places that seemed utterly exotic and out of reach only a few decades ago are now marketed to tourists. The first tourists have been in space, although space tourists reportedly resent the "tourism" label. Flights to the North Pole are offered to the public for $18,000 dollars—or $24,000 if an overnight stay is included.[6] Travel to Antarctica is less expensive, starting at $5,000 dollars, but its attraction as a tourist destination is increasing and the predictions are for substantial growth in the future. There are always new frontiers for those who can afford them; the logic of commercial tourism is committed to making things as convenient as possible for the elites who seek to expand their personal reach.

At the other end of the socioeconomic spectrum, there are many people who travel across the United States on buses because they cannot afford to travel by airplane. Kath Weston has written about her experiences on the road with America's poor.[7] Obstacles in this sort of travel are not the physical frontiers of immense distance and space, and they have nothing to do with the availability of luxurious accommodations. Obstacles are of a different sort, including random inspections by police searching for illegal immigrants and harsh treatment for anyone who even remotely fits the profile. Obstacles also include bus stops that are tucked away in the poorer parts of town, from which it is often difficult to reach the centers. One woman riding the bus sums up the real-life tensions of traveling with limited funds: "Here I am . . . , talking about how lucky I am to live in a rich country, and I can't even afford to buy my lunch!"[8]

Traveling by bus, Weston finds, gives access to "one of the last quasi-public spaces in the United States where people talk, fuss, and fight about corporate finance and household budgets without waiting for some pollster to formulate a decent question."[9] Unfortunately, encounters that are common for passengers on buses traveling long distances hardly take place in the public transportation systems in big cities, whether you find yourself on the metro in Moscow, Buenos Aires, New York City, London or Berlin. My children, when they were young, learned quickly that it is not appropriate to communicate with strangers in these places and that it is best to conduct one's own conversations, if they are necessary at all, in a hushed voice.

Perhaps the most important insight Weston gains in conversations with her fellow travelers on cross-country buses is that terms like "rich" and "poor" are misleading because they cover up the relationship between these groups.[10] Wealth and lack of wealth are not independent phenomena in a situation where the wealth of a few is maintained by low wages for the many. Like many other inequalities, these relationships are more difficult to see from above and are thus best viewed from below.

As a result, the experiences of bus travelers differ dramatically from the scripted encounters of tourists who frequent the commercial worlds of theme parks, resorts and cruises. Bus travelers are most likely aware of those who have the luxury of flying overhead, while air travelers may never have wasted a thought about what low-budget travel on the ground feels like. Furthermore, passengers on long-distance buses are likely to encounter the various forms of travel discussed in this book all at once, from tourism to migration and from vagabonding to mission trips and pilgrimage.

So does travel broaden the horizon? Yes and no. It all depends on whether we allow encounters with other people and with the environment to challenge us. Since travel never takes place in a vacuum, these encounters are inevitable, even for tourists. However, they are scripted and predetermined to varying degrees by the powers that be. The protocols of how to interact with other people, as modeled by the dominant culture, often provide the filter for travelers' experiences, especially in places still considered "exotic." As anthropologist Dennison Nash has observed, "The tourist, like the trader, the employer, the conqueror, the governor, the educator, or the missionary, is seen as the agent of contact between cultures and, directly or indirectly, the cause of change particularly in the less developed regions of the world."[11] Tourists may have somewhat more freedom— and less power—than traders, employers and conquerors. Nevertheless, their encounters with others still mirror the paradigms developed by those other travelers and their power. In other words, as power sets the stage for how the different worlds relate, the tourist is never completely outside of these power relations.

Horizons are broadened effectively only when the lives of travelers and tourists are changed. Yet even for the many tourists today who seek life-changing experiences, change is more likely to happen to the locals. Research has shown a surprising and troublesome paradox: in the encounter between supposedly "unchanging" and "primitive" natives and modern tourists of means who seek a transforming experience, it is often the natives who are forced to change while the tourists stay the same.[12] The natives are the ones who must adapt to the tourists' expectations and ideals in order to stay in business, while the tourists do not even realize what is going on. In this way, relations of imperial power are reinforced in such a way that they permeate all areas of life.[13]

In my experience, this is one of the deepest problems of tourism, which also affects the short-term mission trips that are in vogue with church groups. The unfortunate result is that horizons narrow even though the tourists and mission travelers feel they have broadened. The so-called learning experiences of such trips do not allow for real change on the part of the travelers because they are limited to feeling compassion for the "primitive" and "backwards" locals—an image that exists only in their heads. This misdirected compassion is often combined with a feeling of pride about the travelers' ability to help, without understanding their own place in the relationship.

Horizons will never be broadened, and change cannot happen, unless those who travel begin to understand not only the differences between the two worlds but also the power differentials that are in place. There is, however, hope that some forms of tourism and short-term mission trips foster such insights. When that happens, travelers wake up in their encounters with others and begin to challenge the status quo that controls the lives of travelers and locals alike.

It is this discontent with the status quo that we need to explore further. Even the most privileged and set-in-their-ways tourists are never totally immune to it, and the good news is that many travelers and tourists today aspire to be more than just visitors. Many yearn for a deeper involvement with others and with their cultures and societies in some fashion.[14] In this process, travelers have the opportunity to gain new perspectives on themselves. In a globalizing world it is crucial to gain new perspectives on others and on oneself, as self and others are inextricably related. The individualism invoked by many well-to-do Americans is a myth that covers up the truth that we are connected whether we like it or not. For example, the leather belt I am wearing as I write these lines was produced by the workers in a Mexican *maquiladora* just south of the Arizona border that I visited with a group of students a few years ago. The education of several of my friends in faraway places like Lima and Buenos Aires took place in schools founded by American missionaries in the nineteenth century with the purpose to prepare Latin Americans for participation in US economic ventures. Travel harbors the unique opportunity to become aware of these connections firsthand. Travel becomes revolutionary and transformative when awareness of these connections develops and when the tensions inherent in them inspire and energize change.

In our endeavors to identify challenging travel opportunities, travel books can be of help. But traditional travel books are not very exciting, reading as they do like a strange mix of encyclopedia and phone book. Browsing though pages of facts and descriptions is a boring task made bearable only by colorful pictures of people and places. Even books that describe the adventures and challenges of others are not enough. No, a good travel book will give some space to the tensions produced by the status quo and direct the reader's imagination to possible alternatives. The best travel books acknowledge that travel is nothing without challenges along the way and will therefore enable the reader to travel differently. Such challenges have various components, including getting to know self and others at deeper levels and becoming aware of the tensions that mark our relationships with others.

Gaining a self-critical perspective does not have to be a trite thing, and certain forms of tourism can help us find this out. The ability to laugh at oneself—the humor that great writers like Mark Twain and John Steinbeck were able to put to the page in their travel writings— is a crucial part of this budding self-critical view. Pushing beyond Twain's triad of prejudice, bigotry and narrow-mindedness can enable us to gain a better understanding of power differentials. This is always an option for those who travel with their eyes open.

COMPLEXIFYING MIGRATORY TRAVEL

Along with tourism, a very different kind of travel has been increasing and is also changing the world. As tourism began its ascent after World War II in the United States and Europe, a reverse movement took shape as well, increasingly bringing people from around the world into the centers of wealth and power in the United States and Europe. Migratory travel is an old phenomenon; people have migrated since the beginning of time. What is new, however, is the steadily increasing number of migrants. The massive and growing migrations we witness today are the result of various kinds of tensions. Some of these tensions are of a political nature. People who have been persecuted for political reasons and whose lives are in danger often seek asylum in countries where they are safer. Political persecution has brought many people to Europe and the United States in particular.

The immigration policies of many European countries and of the United States allow for asylum in cases of particular kinds of political persecution. Those whose proofs of political persecution are accepted by the immigration authorities are allowed to stay; others whose proofs are rejected are sent back to their countries of origin, a situation that has created hardship in many cases. According to the United Nations Geneva Convention of 1951, refugee status is granted only on grounds of persecution for reasons of race, religion, nationality or membership of a social group or political opinion; persecution for reasons of gender was added only in the 1990s. Not included in these categories, however, are reasons related to experiences of economic hardship.

Migratory travel for economic reasons is highly controversial both in Europe and the United States. Whereas political refugees are often admired for their integrity and courage, economic refugees can be seen as duplicitous and opportunistic. A common sentiment in Europe and the United States is that political refugees are faced with life-and-death situations; economic refugees, by contrast, are still often considered shallow freeloaders. Such economic refuges, it is assumed, cross borders simply because they want to make more money and live more comfortable lives. In this climate, economic refugees are not even recognized as refugees; rather, they are classified as "illegal immigrants" or, to use a slightly more politically correct term, "undocumented immigrants." The truth is that the lines separating the various reasons for migratory travel are much less clear than is frequently thought.

It is commonly understood that millions of migrants in today's world are following the flow of money, even if this means they have to cross borders. What is less commonly understood, however, is that most migratory travels are anything but voluntary. A closer look reveals that migrants often have little choice whether to travel or not, because they live in situations where they are no longer able to make a living at home. Conversations with migrant travelers along the US-Mexico border, for instance, have helped some of my students understand this often-unacknowledged fact. A large number of the migrants with whom we talked during immersion trips to the border in recent years came from the state of Chiapas, Mexico, where they were pushed off their own lands by multinational corporations. Many of these migrants did not have the option to stay at home. Another reason for migration is the North

American Free Trade Agreement (NAFTA), which has allowed US farmers to sell their corn at such low prices that many Mexican farmers lost their livelihood. If we recognize that political refugees are confronted with life-and-death situations, we need to realize that the same is increasingly true for economic refugees.

These forced travels of migration remind us of a paradox that marks our age: while money is allowed to travel ever more freely across borders in the wake of an increasing number of free-trade agreements, the movements of people who are trying to survive are increasingly restricted. At a time when NAFTA is celebrated and projected to be extended around the world through other similar trade agreements, fences continue to be built along the US-Mexico border. Those migrants who still attempt to cross from Mexico into the United States, following the flow of money mostly out of necessity, are risking their lives to ever greater degrees. In 2012, deaths along the US-Mexico border spiked 27 percent. The death toll keeps growing despite a declining number of people who make it across the border.[15]

It is also often overlooked that the majority of migrants do not head for wealthy countries. The largest numbers of migrants travel within the so-called "intra-periphery" countries of the world, and the second-largest numbers travel within wealthy countries. Only the third place is occupied by migrants who travel between periphery and center. Newly industrializing countries like India, China and Brazil have a lot of internal travel, mostly from rural to urban areas. A more recent labor-related phenomenon in the wealthiest countries is outsourcing, which reduces immigration of men from poorer countries, while work in the domestic sector (such as care for children and the elderly, as well as domestic labor) increases, so that immigrant women are more in demand. These women are in positions of closer relations to the host families than male workers ever were.[16] Migratory travel is thus a complex matter, and each group of migrants has its own experiences. If we want to learn from migration, especially as religious communities who seek to be supportive, we need to learn from the whole story.

My own experience too is that of an immigrant, and my reasons for migrating are just as complex as those of many others, including family reasons as well as the relatively rare opportunity to establish my work in liberation theology at major universities. While migrating from Germany to the United States did not expose me to the same hardships that many other migrants face, this sort of travel is still very different from tourism. Issues like dealing with a foreign culture and language, which tourists sometimes enjoy and sometimes find cumbersome, suddenly become matters of survival. Growing up in the woods of Southern Germany had prepared me early on for the necessity to communicate in idioms different from my mother tongue. So-called *Hochdeutsch* (High German) was substantially different from the local dialects we spoke at home, and evaluations of intellectual competence were often made on the basis of who could speak it best.

The need to communicate effectively in an entirely different language adds considerable difficulties to the experience of travel. While tourists have the freedom to laugh about miscommunicating and misreading people, migrants' fortunes depend on not making too many mistakes. As one of the deans of a prominent theological faculty said to me during a job interview, "We like your work; we just want to see how well you speak English." In my case, many years of studying English in school prepared me for such situations better than many other migrants, who have no choice but to learn as they go. Another difference between tourism and migration is that while most tourists have more power than their hosts, most migrants have considerably less.

Nevertheless, we should not assume that migrants are without power, as migrant communities are changing their hosts' neighborhoods. From new hybrid cultural forms and emerging communication networks produced by migrant communities revolutionary potential arises. Tourism scholar Dean MacCannell talks about a "post-tourist" or "composite community."[17] It may not be an accident that many areas of critical theory, including postcolonialism and subaltern studies, emerged during times of increasing migration.

The complexity of migratory travel increases when we consider different contexts. In the United States, for example, immigrant communities have existed since the first Europeans arrived. The idea that new arrivals of immigrants over the years changed the character of the country is nothing new, and although many of the earlier immigrants came from Europe, these transformations never took place without tension. Migratory travel continues to bring change today. In states such as Texas, immigrants from south of the border now make up the largest minority groups, while the percentage of Caucasians is gradually falling below 50 percent. Of course, there are other groups of Latinos in Texas who have resided in the state since before it was called Texas. As a result, there are many neighborhoods in Texas where Spanish is the preferred language. Perhaps the best gauge of the pervasiveness of these changes is the language on advertising billboards.

The experience of migratory travelers is becoming increasingly elaborate. Advances in transportation and better electronic communications allow these travelers to maintain not only multiple identities but multiple localities as well. "Migrants and refugees develop new, globally oriented identities and pluri- or trans-local understandings of 'home,'" note anthropologists Nadje Al-Ali and Khalid Koser. As a result, "'home' has become a space, a community created within the changing links between 'here' and 'there.'"[18] This was different in the earlier days of migration, when the challenges associated with communication and travel made it much more difficult to maintain contact with home. Even as recently as two or three decades ago talking on the phone was still outrageously expensive. For migratory travelers and refugees today, however, the mythical images of home as a static place that undergird dominant forms of patriotism and nationalism make little sense. This does not mean that notions of home disappear, but there are now a variety of places that become home at the same time. The location of home might also be in the tensions between the country of origin and the country of residence.

As a dual citizen, I can relate to these dynamics and sense how things are shifting. It is noteworthy that the early Christians held similar sentiments. In the letter to the Hebrews, the author puts it this way: "Here we have no lasting city, but we are looking for the city that is to come" (Heb 13:14). Much like contemporary migrants, the early Christians lived in the midst of tensions in their world. They resisted Roman patriotism and nationalism because of their allegiance to the way of Christ, which was not merely a pious idea of the future or the afterlife but a reality embodied in their communities here and now. As Al-Ali and Koser observe, "One of the defining characteristics of transnational migrants is that they have multiple allegiances to places."[19] Yet it seems that these early Christians had their priorities straight, and my own experience testifies to the fact that this is still an option for migrants at present.

Today, an additional aspect of the migratory travel movement is the fact that migrant remittances are increasingly important for the economic well-being of the migrants' families and countries of origin. This reminds us that migrants are never disconnected from their places of origin, much the same as travelers and tourists are never disconnected from their places of origin. More importantly yet, remittances also remind us that migrants continue to shape what is going on in their places of origin. There is no clearer example for my point that travel is always a relational matter and a place where power differentials can and must be negotiated.

Seeing Travel from Two Perspectives

Some fundamental differences between migrants and tourists can now be seen in a clearer perspective. Most tourists expect to return home safely, assuming that their homes are waiting for them. Migrants, on the other hand, often have no such expectations. In the words of MacCannell, "The true heroes are those who leave home not knowing where they will end up, never knowing whether their eventual end will connect meaningfully to their origins, knowing only that their future will be made of dialogue with their fellow travelers and those they meet along the way."[20] This is a more existential form of travel to which any of us who have bought a one-way ticket can relate, one that resembles many of the travels in the Judeo-Christian traditions. Deep lessons for faith and life grow out of this experience, which MacCannell puts in the following words:

> The neo-nomad deeply understands that political promises that pre-suppose or support stability, stasis, the state, real estate, can never be kept. The earth, the ground, only appears to provide reference points for the sedentary. Its true character is to shift endlessly underfoot. What is called "real" as in "real estate" is only what has been privatized; that which is closed to the person or what closes in around the person. As opposed to nomadic freedom, the privatized and the "real" set absolute limits on thought and behavior.[21]

The freedom of the migratory traveler should, of course, not be romanticized. The old advice to be careful what one wishes for applies here above all else. Still, the experiences of migratory travelers can provide much-needed correctives not only for those who stay put but also for those who travel only as tourists.

The travels of the well-to-do tourist, in contrast to the travels of the migrant, can become an "homage to territoriality" and, as Mac-

Cannell continues in his incisive prose, this way to travel "involves elaborate mobile contrivances and temporary accommodations which are designed to mock-up not merely sedentary existence but a kind of ultra-sedentary existence once the province of royalty. Every bourgeois tourist hotel promises to treat its bourgeois guests as 'royalty.' The appeal is to a particular ideal of travel in which the meals, the accommodations, the mode of conveyance, etc., should be more sumptuous, more elaborate and over-prepared than their counterparts at home."[22] These pretensions of the privileged tourist constitute a relationship from the top down, where tourists display their superiority, making it clear that the locals will always fall short. In this sort of tourism, the locals have no choice but to become subservient to the wishes of the tourists if they want to survive. MacCannell observes two emerging poles. On the one hand, migratory travelers embody "a new synthetic arrangement of life which releases human creativity." Those tourist travelers who represent the establishment, on the other hand, embody "a new form of authority, containment of creativity, and control."[23]

There is a difference between what has been called "transnationalism from above and from below,"[24] and travelers, tourists and migrants all fit somewhere in this dichotomy. While transnationalism from above describes dominant globalization where the elite expand their power across the globe, transnationalism from below describes the sort of relationships where common people—the multitude[25]—develop their own agency. Many migrant communities are already embodying this agency but, as we shall see, even nonmigratory travelers and tourists have an opportunity to align themselves with these alternative powers.

three

Pilgrims and Vagabonds

Challenges from the Road

Pɪʟɢʀɪᴍᴀɢᴇ, ᴠᴀɢᴀʙᴏɴᴅɪɴɢ ᴀɴᴅ ᴛᴏᴜʀɪsᴍ are ways of travel that have distinct histories but often seem to overlap in the contemporary world. Tourism in particular is broad and diverse enough that it can include some of the other forms of traveling. Nevertheless, there is something distinctive about pilgrimage and vagabonding that is worth investigating, especially in light of our explorations of a short theology of travel and justice. Let us begin with a closer look at pilgrimage and then move on to vagabonding.

Pɪʟɢʀɪᴍᴀɢᴇ

Sociologist of religion Luigi Tomasi defines pilgrimage as a religious search for the divine, "a journey undertaken for religious purposes that culminates in a visit to a place considered to be the site or manifestation of the supernatural—a place where it is easier to obtain divine help."[1] Others, seeking to erase some of the sharp distinctions between pilgrimage and tourism, have argued that travel in search of authenticity and self-renewal also constitutes a search for the sacred and should thus also be understood as a form of pilgrimage.[2] Further broadening the understanding of pilgrimage in the present, arguments have been made that pilgrimage today includes even travels to popular shrine-like places such as Graceland, Tennessee, the home of Elvis Presley. A short history of pilgrimage will help us understand why pilgrimage might still be of interest to us, even though its meaning continues to erode as it is assimilated into tourism.

Pilgrimages originated as forms of itinerant devotion in the seventh century CE in Western Christendom. The number of these itinerant devotions kept growing and peaked in the twelfth and thirteenth centuries. Pilgrimages in those periods were seen as a "major investment in eternal life."[3] The use of economic language, describing pilgrimages as an investment, reflects the cultural assumptions of those eras because religion, politics and economics were not considered the separate phenomena that they are now. Everything was at stake in these travels: not only religion but also politics and economics. Pilgrimage affected all of these realms, not only in the lives of the travelers themselves but also in the broader religious, political and economic contexts of the communities where the travelers lived.

As far as individual travelers were concerned, pilgrimages were dangerous and risky undertakings. Many things had to be given up and others were lost along the road, and often travelers did not return home. But even if everything went according to plan for individual travelers, there were political and social consequences that could not be avoided. A pilgrimage could be considered as something akin to a "civil death," because it put the pilgrims outside of the structures of their communities and societies. According to medieval law, pilgrims were declared physically dead if they had not been heard of for a year and a day.

While physical death was a constant companion of life for pilgrims in the Middle Ages, the pilgrims' bigger concern was for what they considered spiritual death. To contemporary ears, this may sound like a simple trade of one world for another (the heavenly world for the physical world), but we should not overlook the implications of the fact that these pilgrims intentionally gave up the securities of the political and economic status quo to the point of confronting physical death. These acts of giving up imply a defiance of the physical world that must have left its mark, as the physical world was not brushed aside but put in its place. A pilgrim would have intuitively understood that life is more than what the status quo can offer and promise. In other words, giving up the physical world of the status quo would have empowered pilgrims to envision not only the heavenly world but also an alternative physical world where the rules of the status quo were challenged.

At the end of the Middle Ages, pilgrimage underwent important changes. As modernity emphasized the freedom of the individual and helped fund this freedom for the elites through the economic developments associated with budding capitalism, pilgrimages could now also be undertaken as a demonstration of freedom and personal independence. As a result, in the seventeenth and eighteenth centuries pilgrimages often took shape as the travels of educated elites who set out to view examples of fine art and other cultural artifacts of interest. In the nineteenth and twentieth centuries, the development of tourism further changed the understanding of pilgrimage, as sightseeing, tourism and pilgrimage were increasingly combined and made available to broader groups of people.

Today, whatever contradictions remain between travel for the purposes of enjoyment and travel for reasons of faith have been further eroded as the tourism industry has taken over. Nevertheless, although most contemporary pilgrimages are now organized along the lines of mass tourism, some claim that the purpose of these pilgrimages is still similar to the purpose of pilgrimages in the old days: to seek the sacred.

What has changed over the years, of course, are not just the forms of pilgrimage but also popular definitions of the sacred and how people relate to it. Where once the pilgrim's search for the sacred implied a challenge and had to do with concepts like penitence and an intentional commitment to the hardships and dangers of the journey, now the search for the sacred is more likely connected to concepts like personal growth and self-realization. Where once the search for the sacred implied a search for how best to conform to it, now the search for the sacred tends to imply the assumption that the sacred conforms to the interests of the pilgrim, affirming (or perhaps improving) the status quo rather than challenging it.

In addition, the hardships and dangers of the journey have been reduced to such an extent by modern forms of travel that the journey itself has been all but abandoned as a meaningful part of most pilgrimages. What matters most today are arrival and departure. Tomasi describes the World Youth Rally in Rome on August 20, 2000, which attracted 2.5 million young people, with these words: "The stone used as a pillow, typical of the pilgrim of the past and symbolic of penitence, had given way to the cellular phone, the paramount symbol of comfort in the modern age."[4] Modern-day pilgrims may not even be aware that things have ever been different.

The relinquishment of the more challenging aspects of an encounter with the sacred—aspects characteristic of the historical purposes of pilgrimage—is paralleled by a certain domestication of the sacred in contemporary religiosity. Modern pilgrims assume the approval of the sacred and are interested in how they can better integrate the sacred with their own concerns, while ancient pilgrims would have assumed the difference of the sacred, seeking to adjust their concerns to the concerns of the sacred. This is similar to the difference between wondering whether God is on our side (the typical quest of modernity and of those who benefit from its political and economic structures) and whether we are on God's side (the quest of those who understand that things are not as they should be, which today is also the quest of various liberation and postcolonial theologies).[5]

In this climate it is not hard to see that trying to recover some of the challenging aspects of traditional pilgrimages would benefit those who seek to reclaim their faith on the road. Yet the death-defying attitudes of medieval pilgrims are not easily reclaimed by the contemporary traveler who has access not only to travel insurance and cell phones but also to an industry that is designed to defray the challenges of travel. At the same time, since the exigencies of travel can never be completely controlled, travel might still be one of the better opportunities for well-to-do contemporaries to open up and to broaden their horizons.

A first step toward reclaiming the traditional challenges of pilgrimage might be to gain a better awareness of what happens when the world of the pilgrim is put in touch with other worlds, however limited these experiences might be for contemporary pilgrims. Anthropologist Victor Turner's concept of liminality might be helpful here, referring to a situation of finding oneself in between different worlds. Liminality, which means being on the threshold or on the border, has the potential to challenge established hierarchies and can thus create space for new kinds of relationship and perhaps even for the sacred itself.[6]

Literary scholar Walter Mignolo's notion of border thinking pushes this experience of liminality to the next level, exploring what happens when people find themselves in border situations where various worlds collide in tension and conflict. The question of power differentials is of particular importance here, because those who find themselves on the marginalized sides of these borders are best positioned to see both sides in new light. These marginalized voices also have some potential to formulate the resulting challenges to the status quo.[7] Pilgrims who are open to examining their positions of power and who are willing to move closer to the margins might have an opportunity to share in these alternative perspectives.

The fact that traditional places of pilgrimage are often located in remote places further supports the potential benefits of pilgrimage. Those pilgrims who have the nerve to venture further off the beaten path might even encounter some aspects of hybridity—the fused nature of identity that welds together dominant and repressed aspects of life in one person. Hybridity is a crucial part of the experience of colonized peoples and those who have come under pressure from the dominant system.[8] These experiences not only help to examine, challenge and destabilize the selves of the privileged; they also enable fresh encounters with other people and ultimately the divine Other, who are all kept at arm's length by the status quo.

Pilgrimage is an image that has sometimes been invoked when Christians have understood that assimilating to the status quo was not an option. The text of the following hymn was written during the time of the Third Reich in Germany by Christians who refused to go along with the fascist status quo, which determined not only culture and politics but also the Christianity of the time.

> We are but guests on earth, wandering toward the eternal home restlessly, enduring many hardships.

> Our paths are deserted and often we are alone. In these grey alleyways no one wants to accompany us.

> The only one walking with us is dear Christ; he walks by our side when all others forsake us.

> Many paths lead out of this world. Oh that we may we not lose the way to our parental home.

> And when at last we get tired, put out a light for us, oh God in your grace, so that we will find the way home.[9]

What may sound like an expression of sentimental feelings of lone-liness and abandonment reflects the experience of those who have mustered the courage of medieval pilgrims to step outside of the religious, political and economic status quo and to take a stance against it. This hymn is written by Christians who are ready to bear the consequences for their defiance against a dominant system that claims Christianity and God for itself. Perhaps this was the reason my father and some of the older people in the Southern German Methodist church where I grew up remembered it so well.

Christians in the United States today may find this theology dif-ficult to relate to, because experiences of resistance against the status quo have little room in the dominant forms of Christianity. Affirmation of the status quo rather than challenge is the goal, and neither conservative nor liberal mainliners worry much about as-similation to the status quo of our times. Just the opposite: religion is often seen as that which upholds the dominant ways of life, that which people have come to accept as normal. In the United States, the experience of the excluded—whether for reasons of race, class, gender or even sexuality—can help us understand what it means to stay the course of our journey. This is particularly important when the status quo blocks the roads for those who are different, forces us to travel the alleyways and secondary roads and sometimes dis-courages travel altogether if it is not able to trivialize the travel experience. The status quo, even in faith communities, rarely en-courages truly life-changing travel experiences.

One of the key challenges of any pilgrimage is having to leave the familiar places of home, of family and friends, and to forgo the af-firmation of familiar religious communities. Yet, especially as Christians who have grown comfortable with the status quo, we desperately need such reminders that we are not in control, and we need to understand that none of our familiar places must ever assume the place of God. The Christian God is not the God of the familiar but the God who calls us to embark on journeys that model and prefigure the struggles of life. This journey ultimately points us to our true home, which is found at last where we least expect it: in the presence of God, who is often encountered in special ways in the unfamiliar, exemplified for Christians in the life, death and resurrection of Jesus Christ, the Jesus who walked the dusty roads of Galilee in the past and who continues to walk the alleyways and secondary roads today.

This challenge is deepened further in Christ's presence at the margins of society, as expressed in the words of Jesus in the Gospel of Matthew that keep haunting self-centered Christianity: "Truly I tell you, just as you did it to one of the least of these who are members of my family, you did it to me" (Mt 25:40). As we have learned in chapter one, this concern is not as unusual as many Christians might think, as it reverberates throughout many of the books of the Bible.

To be sure, leaving familiar places is not merely an act of deconstruction. For the vagrants and hermits of the Middle Ages, "their pilgrimage to God was an exercise in self-construction," notes sociologist Zygmunt Bauman.[10] People moving out of their established homes also moved out of the religious, political and economic control of the status quo and found alternative visions and constructed new ways of life. The established church resented these movements because it wanted to be the only connection to God, and it thus tried to organize these vagrants into monastic orders. Yet the challenges posed to the status quo by the pilgrims proved too strong, so the powers that be were never completely able to control them.

In a postmodern context, where lives are often no longer as grounded in traditional relationships as they once were, some have argued that pilgrimage has become a way of life. Rootedness in families, traditional communities and geographical locations can no longer be presupposed as a given. This may be linked to the fact that the economic security many members of the middle classes once took for granted is now becoming more and more elusive. Bauman notes that even one of the foremost strategies of pilgrimage, "saving for the future,"[11] makes less and less sense as pension plans and 401(k) plans fail us.

More than a century ago Karl Marx described this feeling of being lost and suspended in time and space in his own way, reminding us of the underlying cause that Bauman does not address, namely a capitalism that constantly needs to reinvent itself in order to stay competitive: "Constant revolutionising of production, uninterrupted disturbance of all social conditions, everlasting uncertainty and agitation distinguish the bourgeois epoch from all earlier ones. All fixed, fast-frozen relations, with their train of ancient and venerable prejudices and opinions, are swept away, all new-formed ones become antiquated before they can ossify." Marx's famous conclusion is well-known to people steeped in continental philosophy: "All that is solid melts into air, all that is holy is profaned, and man is at last compelled to face with sober senses his real conditions of life, and his relations with his kind."[12] What jet-setting business traveler, and even some of us jet-setting Christians, could not relate to the disturbing feeling that all that is solid melts into air?

In this context, as poststructuralist philosophy has taught us, meaning is never fixed but is shaped in relationship. According to Bauman, "The pilgrim and the desert-like world he walks acquire their meanings *together*, and *through each other*."[13] When seen in light of Marx's challenge, however, Bauman's description is too general. Even in a postmodern context, relationships are never as open-ended as they might seem. Capitalism is not a matter of open-ended relationships, as some tend to believe; rather, capitalism is structured in such a way that one class builds its wealth and power on the back of another class. This is hard to deny at a time when it is generally taken for granted that the rich get richer and the poor get poorer. This is the context in which more and more people are beginning to wake up, as it is when the pretensions of seemingly stable traditions melt away that people can see their "real conditions of life" and "[their] relations with [their] kind."

Most importantly, in this context pilgrims might be the ones who resist "melting into air" and who keep seeking an alternative, "saving for an alternative future." In this way they defy the future projected by the capitalist economy and create an alternative vision connected to an alternative way of life.

VAGABONDING

Bauman's description of the lot of pilgrims—wandering without being grounded in any one place—might better fit the experience of vagabonds. Vagabonds, Bauman notes, are people without a master, free to move. Modernity despised them because vagabonds claimed the freedom to move and resisted order and control. As a result, they were even more unpredictable than pilgrims. In modern times there were few vagabonds; in postmodernity there are many, as there are fewer and fewer places to which people truly belong.

To be sure, no travelers, whether vagabonds, pilgrims, migrants or tourists, ever really belong to the places they visit. Nevertheless, tourists who have some financial means can afford to maintain a safe distance from the things they experience: "In the tourist's world, the strange is tame, domesticated, and no longer frightens; shocks come in a package deal with safety," Bauman notes.[14] In this way, well-to-do tourists, sharing in the fluidity of postmodernity while riding mostly the top waves of capitalism, make sure that the world will serve their desire and that they will be able to control it to some degree. The shocks that vagabonds experience, in contrast, are rarely softened by the cushions of capital. Well-heeled tourists, like capitalists, have choices that vagabonds, who typically travel on a shoestring like migrant workers and even struggling middle class travelers, do not have.

If it is true that the experience of the sacred is connected to an experience of being challenged—a truth the pilgrims of past centuries knew intuitively—it may well be that vagabonds come closer to this experience. Vagabonds might come closer to the sacred than even contemporary pilgrims, who have the luxury of availing themselves of the amenities of mass tourism. Whereas many contemporary pilgrims seek self-affirmation and self-realization and are willing and able to pay for the privilege, vagabonds may well be the ones who stand a better chance of experiencing the shocks of the sacred. Of course, vagabonds may not call their experience by that name, but it is real nonetheless.

Like pilgrimage, vagabonding has a long history. In the Europe of past centuries, vagabonds were people who were forced to move from one place to another in order to make a living. They were considered *herrenlos* (without a master) and thus unreliable, dangerous and probably godless as well. Vagabonds included the lowest level of workers as well as those that today would be considered migratory workers. Aspiring craftsmen learning a trade would often do their apprenticeships on the road as well, traveling from one town to the next, although they would consider themselves *ehrbar* (honorable) and thus did not identify with vagabonds.

Nevertheless, traveling apprentices often gave expression to the same experiences as vagabonds. Some of their traditions lament having to leave home and loved ones, but the other half of their traditions celebrate the resulting freedom and independence. An old German folk song has the apprentice say these words to the master after describing a number of subversive acts carried out by apprentices: "I tell him freely to his face that I do not appreciate his wages and his work. I will try my luck and march on."[15] Even if the apprentice was not without a master permanently, the experience of being without a master temporarily appears to have been a powerful and transformative one.

A new type of vagabond has featured prominently in American literature of the twentieth century, and these experiences provide some important insights for us as well. Vagabonding in the America after the 1940s often attracted young people who sought freedom and older people tired of tourist schemes, where money and status guaranteed mindless comfort and safety. Most of these vagabonds were not without means, but they were willing to renounce the privilege that came with money. Those who learn that one can travel in simpler ways are often the ones who also come to understand what most people never realize: namely that it is possible to live one's life in alternative fashion and in simpler ways.

Perhaps the most famous vagabond in the United States is Jack Kerouac, whose book *On the Road* has become an icon. Yet the vagabond story told by this Beat poet is not the story of a slacker, as is often assumed. Sal, the hero of Kerouac's book, is willing to work and contribute to society. Sal is not willing, however, to work for work's sake. The distinction he draws is between authentic work and the work people do in order to become consumers of stuff. Sal, according to literary critic John Leland, "rejects upward mobility as a plot to make men do pointless things, turning them into parodies of the American Dream."[16] What enables Sal to work and to write is moving down the ladder of success rather than up. Vagabonding— getting out from under the status quo, being on the road—helps him accomplish this goal of moving down.

Like the pilgrims of old, vagabonding Sal steps out of the religious, social and economic status quo quite deliberately. Kerouac has him say these words: "The only people for me are the mad ones, the ones who are mad to live, mad to talk, mad to be saved, desirous of everything at the same time, the ones who never yawn or say a commonplace thing, but burn, burn, burn like fabulous yellow roman candles exploding like spiders across the stars and in the middle you see the blue centerlight and everybody goes 'Awww!'"[17]

Sal's trips are ultimately about these mad but at the same time fully alive people. Vagabonding helps him draw a line between the mad people and those who have bought into the status quo to such a degree that all alternatives have disappeared: "In Davenport, Iowa, somehow all the cars were farmer-cars, and once in a while a tourist car, which is worse, with old men driving and their wives pointing out the sights or poring over maps, and sitting back looking at everything with suspicious faces."[18] Vagabonds experience the world in ways tourists never will. This holds true for the sacred as well: it escapes those who seek to control it, to be experienced by those who are willing to embrace what is different.

Another prominent vagabond in American literature is John Steinbeck. In *Travels with Charley*, Steinbeck embarks on an extended trip around the United States accompanied by his French standard poodle Charley but not by his wife. His reason for traveling by himself is simple: "Two or more people disturb the ecologic complex of an area. I had to go alone and I had to be self-contained."[19] For his travels, he uses a pickup truck with a camper shell on the back, driving mostly on back roads and off the beaten path. Steinbeck's rationale for traveling alone pays off: across the country, he encounters many people who share with him the sorts of thoughts and feelings that pushed below the surface. Vagabonding has to do with these rare connections to other people rather than with the vagabond's ego. Despite his status as a famous writer, Steinbeck steps back from his prominent status and, in the process, is never recognized on the entire trip.[20]

After vagabonding through the United States for several months, camping out in fields, in forests and on farms, Steinbeck concludes, "We find after years of struggle that we do not take a trip; a trip takes us. . . . Only when this is recognized can the blown-in-the-glass bum relax and go along with it. Only then do the frustrations fall away. In this a journey is like a marriage. The certain way to be wrong is to think you control it."[21] Vagabonds differ from tourists and from all those who stay at home in that they relinquish control over their experiences. Rather than embarking on a journey, they become part of the journey, and if things go well, they are transformed by the experience.

Steinbeck finds in his travels that almost all Americans have a burning desire to be on the move. Much of this desire still exists in our own time. But since people are busier than ever, struggling to make ends meet, they often settle for short trips with as many amenities as possible; perhaps this is why cruise ships are becoming more and more popular. Vagabonding is a different way to deal with the desire to travel. Steinbeck recalls knowing "that ten or twelve thousand miles driving a truck, alone and unattended, over every kind of road, would be hard work." But he sees this as "the antidote for the poison of the professional sick man. And in my own life I am not willing to trade quality for quantity."[22] What if this professional sickness, the inability to distance ourselves from whatever the status quo imposes on us and the inability to conceive of alternatives—including the sacred—could indeed be addressed by vagabonding? The status quo seems to be worried about this, so its representatives seek to ensure that people increasingly drown in their work and miss what is truly important in life. There is a lesson here for people of faith.

Steinbeck's return home exemplifies an experience that many vagabonds share. When he finally returns from his journey, he ends up making a wrong turn and stops his truck. When a police officer approaches, Steinbeck responds, "Officer, I've driven this thing all over the country—mountains, plains, deserts. And now I'm back in my own town, where I live—and I'm lost."[23] Getting lost at home, having to explore again familiar locations, may be one of the most important aspects of vagabonding. When people of faith engage in vagabonding experiences, as well as immersions and short-term mission trips discussed in the next chapter, they often return with the ability to explore familiar theologies and communities in new ways.

The spirit of vagabonding is sometimes best captured in books that do not have a place in the canon of great literary works. Motorcycle travelers often get closer to the people on the road than those who travel in cars; perhaps they are helped by the fact that they are seen as less privileged and wealthy. Lois Pryce, a single woman who took off from work in Britain to travel the Americas from north to south for ten months on a small motorcycle, sums up her experiences: "What I hadn't bargained for was how the motorcycle encouraged friendliness, curiosity from strangers that would inevitably turn into something more—an offer of hospitality, practical assistance or just some words of encouragement when I needed them most."[24]

This level of exposure to people is bought with a lack of comfort and security, an exposure to the elements of the weather and geography and to the road and its dangers. Most people are unwilling to endure this, and they usually let the motorcycle traveler know that they consider his or her journey madness or suicide. Of course, those of us who use bikes for daily transportation know what I am talking about, as everybody everywhere in every moment reminds us of the dangers of riding. Here is a place where the mad people that Kerouac's Sal seeks out merge with those who dare to travel in unconventional ways.

Pryce shares the common experience of vagabonds that it is not possible to control the trip but that the trip takes over: the trip literally takes them. Vagabonds who set out with a touristic intention to see the world and the sights often find that something else takes over. Pryce concludes, "More than the countries and the towns and the scenery of the last ten months, it was the people that had brought my trip to life."[25] She did not expect this to happen.

The motorcycle travels of Dave Barr push the limits of the possible. A veteran with two amputated legs, Barr rides a two-wheeled

motorcycle around the world.[26] Barr works against incredible
physical odds, as he is also without hearing in one of his ears. His
write-up of his experiences is raw and unfiltered, telling how he got
on with two artificial limbs and had to deal with the fragile me-
chanics of an old Harley-Davidson motorcycle, a chronic lack of
money and a large number of breakdowns. Yet Barr's experiences
also show that vagabonding does not always put aside the most
cherished prejudices of Americans. Today Barr gives talks about
faith and success, yet one wonders how it is possible to maintain the
typical American notion of individual success and "pulling yourself
up by your bootstraps" in light of his adventures as a disabled motorcycle traveler who had to be picked up many times by others. Barr
owes his life to relationships with the often-underprivileged people
who saved him time after time. Would not the success of a disabled
motorcycle vagabond redefine any notion of what can be considered
success? Why is it so hard to get a glimpse of the divine in the
trenches? Do we have no other option than envisioning the divine
at the top, with those whom we consider successful?

One of the most famous motorcycle travel stories is, of course,
that of Che Guevara. His travels through Latin America with a
friend, Alberto Granado, on a faltering motorcycle lead to a conversion experience. The diary he keeps of this journey contains the
many small details that vagabonds experience on the road. Along
the way, Guevara moves closer to the common people of the con-
tinent and begins to understand the sources of their plight. Encounters with miners in Chile awaken his consciousness. He learns
that he and Granado are the rare exceptions who ask the guide
about how many lives were lost in the mines rather than about the
impressive technology employed.

Meeting many others who struggle to make a living contributes
to Guevara's eventual conversion from a middle-class medical
student who wants to contribute to the good of humanity to a

person who is no longer able to tolerate the injustices and inequalities responsible for producing so much human suffering. What Guevara gradually realizes on his journey, and what we can learn whether or not we agree with his eventual conclusions, is that human suffering and struggle as it presents itself today is not a natural catastrophe. We are up against manmade powers that may be even more powerful. After all, he notes, the mine owners in Chile prefer to lose thousands of pesos every day in a strike so as not to have to increase the workers' pay for a few centavos.[27]

Walking into a church and listening to a sermon for one and a half hours, Guevara and Granado finally leave after repeated invocations of images of a patient Christ that somehow bring on one of Guevara's asthma attacks.[28] I have to confess that I have on occasion had to leave churches myself during the sermon because of an uncontrollable cough. Anyone who has ever experienced the discrepancy between real suffering and the platitudes of such doctrines will probably understand. The challenge of the sacred is not only missed here, it is carefully covered up by one of the innumerable theologians of the status quo.

In the introduction to his journal, Guevara notes that he is no longer the one who embarked on the journey: "The person who reorganizes and polishes [these notes], me, is no longer, at least I'm not the person I once was. All this wandering around 'Our America with a capital A' has changed me more than I thought."[29] A conversion, in the most genuine sense of the word, has taken place, which is described in the end: "I knew that when the great guiding spirit cleaves humanity into two antagonistic halves, I would be with the people."[30] Is this not where Christ was found as well?

Another motorcyclist who follows Guevara's tracks more than four decades later adds the following insight: "Every long journey overturns the established order of one's own life, and all revolutionaries must begin by transforming themselves."[31] The premise of the author of the famous book *Zen and the Art of Motorcycle Maintenance*,[32] that traveling by car is like watching a movie but riding a motorcycle is like being in one, is trumped in the case of Guevara: riding a motorcycle that eventually breaks down catapults him into the heart of the people, a place from which no one can return unchanged.

One of the bestselling books about vagabonding was written by a young author, Rolf Potts. Potts starts from a position of privilege but raises questions about how privilege is best used: "Vagabonding is about using the prosperity and possibility of the information age to increase your personal options instead of your personal possessions."[33] While this sort of vagabonding suggests detachment from possessions, it still depends on the prosperity produced by modern capitalism. This places the vagabond in a tension that is not easily resolved but might end up being productive. The world of the vagabond is "not the ordinary one, for travel itself, even the most commonplace, is an implicit quest for anomaly."[34] The question for us, unfortunately not raised by Potts, is how the vagabond will make use of the tensions experienced on the road: merely for the purpose of self-help or for the purposes of making a contribution to the common good and the transformation of the world, thus moving closer to the divine?

Like other vagabonds, Potts notes the importance of meeting other people on the road and he explores the way this challenges the traveler: "Much of what's memorable in meeting people from faraway lands is how these interactions wind up teaching you about your own, culture-fed instincts."[35] To be sure, while the teaching takes place regardless of whether anyone pays attention or not, learning does not happen by default. Vagabonds, by virtue of being less able to control their travels, may be more open to learning than tourists. Still, developing truly mutual relationships with others does not happen automatically; it takes some work. If mutual relations that benefit both sides are not built, vagabonds may at times be worse than tourists and worse than those social scientists who travel in order to study the lives of others. In a survey, Australian Aborigines stated that they preferred mass tourists to anthropologists, as the tourists bought their souvenirs and did not ask a lot of questions.[36] Nevertheless, vagabonding, as described by Potts, has the potential to help broaden people's horizons where tourism has failed us.

Vagabonding in some of the forms described here may seem like a luxury. As Rosemarie Henkel-Rieger, my wife, noted when reading these pages, vagabonding may not be an option for everyone, including parents who are busy with their children. Nevertheless, there are families who have done some vagabonding as well.[37] Our own family has spent time on the road on numerous occasions. One of these experiences included a couple of months in South Africa, driving six thousand miles in a small VW Chico—the same car that was sold in the United States as the VW Rabbit or Golf in the 1970s and 1980s—when our twin daughters were twelve years old, living a simple life and meeting many people while I gave lectures at various universities. For us, vagabonding with children has been an especially powerful way of learning that we cannot be in control, and it has exposed our children to the sorts of lessons that parents, teachers and religious professionals could never teach them. Our experiences also confirm that many people are especially open and kind to travelers with smaller children, as such travelers are generally aware of their vulnerability and more likely to be in need of help. Vagabonds with children have to place themselves at the mercy of others in a way that few other travelers would.

One thing adults might learn from children on these travels is how well children can blend in. When my daughters were five years old, one of them returned from a fairly short family trip to Cambridge, England, with a Cambridge accent. In Sheffield, England, our daughters told us we could not leave because they had not made any friends yet. Once they had the opportunity to play with some children at a playground, they were satisfied. In Moscow, a shopkeeper asked my wife and me what we Americans were doing with those two Russian girls, referring to our ten-year-old twin daughters who had blended in much more than we did.

For grownups, the hard work of learning about others may best be accomplished not in the context of leisure but in the context of work. As travel journalist Charles Kuralt advises, "If you really want to learn about a country, work there."[38] Here the circle closes when we look back at the vagabonding workers of the past: not only did they embody some of the freedoms not available to those under the constant tutelage of masters, they also were the ones who could see what was going on at a deeper level—the sorts of things that escape the status quo.

Learning about others in situations of leisure is different from learning when working side by side with someone having to endure the same pressures and even the same boss. Moreover, if God can be compared to a traveler who works rather than to a static deity sitting on a throne, beginning with the hard work of creation (see especially the second creation story, Genesis 2:4-24, where God is a craftsman who forms people and animals from clay and plants a garden and trees), what better place to encounter the divine?

PARALLEL EXPERIENCES

Despite all differences, there are some parallels between the experiences of vagabonds and pilgrims, and these experiences perhaps come together best in Sam Cooke's blues song "A Change Is Gonna Come." The speaker in this song is a vagabond who has had a hard life always on the run. He realizes he can do nothing yet he remains confident that change is going to come.

Neither vagabonds nor pilgrims are ultimately in control. Becoming a pilgrim used to require a relinquishment of connections to the powers that be, and the same is true for vagabonds. Cooke's vagabond, however, finds himself in worse trouble than pilgrims could ever imagine. The cards are stacked against him to such an extent that even the eternal home, to which pilgrims look forward in hope, has been replaced by a question mark. For Cooke's vagabond, not even heaven is a safe option anymore.

This should not be surprising, because the powers that be not only claim this world; they seek to claim any world on which they are able to lay their hands, including the world that is to come. Even pilgrims may find to their surprise that at the end of their journey, the dominant powers are already there. Nevertheless, Cooke's vagabond is hopeful, an inspiration to pilgrims: change is on its way, and it is going to come. Both vagabonds and pilgrims know what the representatives of the status quo do not want them to know: none of the powers that be will last forever, and no empire has ever been here to stay—despite many prominent claims to the contrary.

Potts, not a religious writer, puts his finger on one of the most powerful lessons that vagabonds can learn: "If you travel long enough, you'll find that your spiritual revelations are invariably grounded in the everyday."[39] That God is at work in the everyday is the experience of many of the biblical travelers we discussed in an earlier chapter, and this is one of the lessons that even pilgrims can learn if they take the journey and its many challenges seriously.

four

Beyond Religious Tourism

Short-Term Mission Trips and Immersions Upside-Down

As tourism keeps growing, so does what some have called "religious tourism." Religious tourism shares many of the same opportunities and problems of tourism, yet the problems associated with tourism can be seen more clearly here. As we address and deal with these problems, we might discover the opportunities and find out how to transform and redeem tourism as a whole.

One of the advantages of religious tourism is that those who travel in this way are often more heavily invested in their travels than regular tourists. Self-centered diversions, fun and games are not their primary motivations for travel, and neither is sheer curiosity about that which is different. Let's take a closer look at the purposes of religious tourism.

One of the purposes of religious tourism is to recover things that have been lost at home. In this regard, religious tourists resemble pilgrims in pursuit of the sacred, yet they differ from pilgrims in that they look for religious experiences in other places. They do not necessarily seek out sites of religious prominence, such as shrines or holy sites. Instead, religious tourists often expect to find religious experiences in places that seem to be more "primitive" and thus somehow more "pristine" and "authentic." A common expectation is that in places where people live simpler lives, religious practices are simpler, too, and thus closer to some original state of religious authenticity that matches up with our own past.

Among Christian religious tourists, for instance, there is often an expectation that Christianity in the Southern Hemisphere is not only simpler but also more traditional, heartfelt and authentic than Christianity in the North. Some of these expectations find support even from scholars who assume, often with only superficial evidence, that Christians in the Southern Hemisphere are more traditional than Christians in the North.[1] Hearing an African choir sing old hymns like "What a Friend We Have in Jesus" or "Jesus Loves Me, This I Know" gives many Americans and Europeans a feeling of being transported to the happier religious days of a bygone era. As a result, religious travelers often talk about their faith being invigorated and enriched by this sort of travel.

What they overlook, of course, is that the same texts and words can have different meanings in different contexts. When the slave masters in the United States heard the slaves sing, "Swing low, sweet chariot, coming for to carry me home," for instance, they assumed that the slaves were talking about a disembodied heaven. The slaves, on the other hand, were singing about freedom in this world and the liberation brought by the Underground Railroad. This complexity, understood by the slaves but not by the masters, allowed the slaves to communicate while the masters were sent "away empty" by God, like the rich in Mary's Song of Praise (Lk 1:53).

Another purpose of religious tourism is captured by the familiar discourse of conversion. In earlier periods conversion was usually seen as a one-way street, where religious travelers sought to convert those whom they encountered in their travels. Today, we need to think of conversion in the other direction as well: Is it possible that religious tourists themselves might be converted in the process of traveling?[2]

The ultimate danger here is a theological one: by missing the reality of others and failing to be transformed, we are also missing the reality of God.

Searching for Two-Way Streets

That religious travel can invigorate and enrich the faith of travelers has often been noted and is not in question. This acknowledgment may be considered a compliment to those whom religious travelers encounter on their journeys both at home and abroad. But the language of enrichment points to a problem, as enrichment has also been one of the driving motives of colonial and neocolonial travel. Columbus set out to facilitate trade as he searched for a Western trade route to India; he was in the business of enrichment, as were those who founded the British East India Company in 1600 CE.

Today, business executives and their employees travel for similar reasons, seeking to extend the reach of their companies. One way enrichment happens, for instance, is through the acquisition of raw materials overseas that are refined, manufactured and put to use back home. The list of raw materials has grown in recent years, due to the production of cell phones and computers that require rare metals and minerals. This model from the world of business has surprising parallels in the world of faith. The so-called simple faith of natives has often been used as raw materials by theologians and religious scholars who collect stories of faith and put them to profitable use back home, manufacturing them into sermons and books.

None of us is off the hook in this matter. Even those travelers who consider themselves neutral observers, including journalists and scholars of religion who claim they merely seek to describe and understand the religion of others, are part of the enrichment game.

While journalists and scholars may not get rich off their work, someone else usually benefits from the articles and studies that describe the lives and faith of others in faraway places. Knowledge, as is well-known, is power.

What are generally missing in these situations are two-way relationships where both parties benefit from the encounter and where the winner-take-all mentality is suspended. The fundamental question for us is this: Rather than just being a source of enrichment and grist for the religious or academic mill, how can religious travel challenge and transform the traveler, and how can the hosts benefit as well?

This question is also relevant not only for religious travel but also for what has come to be known as "mission in reverse," or what we might call "religious tourism in reverse." In this form of travel, people from other parts of the globe journey to places of wealth like the United States and Europe in order to proclaim their faith or perform religious services. In these cases, enrichment and invigoration are still the major purposes, yet this time travelers from other parts of the world are expected to enrich and invigorate the faith of Americans and Europeans at home. Genuine two-way relationships are just as scarce in these endeavors as in other forms of tourism, because now the travelers are those with fewer economic means and less power. While the "simple faith" and the "incredible trust in God" of these missionaries in reverse are celebrated, their services are rendered without much of a challenge to anyone.

If "mission in reverse" is truly to make a difference to us, it can happen only when we begin to realize what is really going on in the world. We need to learn and understand who we are in relation to each other, and we need to begin to address the existing power differentials. Unless true mission in reverse is able to break open and transform these power differentials, the one-way street remains and the enrichment of the powerful is the result.

As a theologian, I wonder if God can reach us if we have never experienced the relationship of a two-way street.

The Problems of Short-Term Mission Trips and Immersions

Other popular forms of religious tourism include so-called short-term mission trips offered by an increasing number of churches and immersion courses offered by many theological schools and seminaries. Before we take a look at the tremendous opportunities of these sorts of travel, we need to become aware of their inherent problems. Some of these problems are so serious that a number of scholars have advised that the church discontinue mission trips and immersions altogether, and some prominent schools of theology have canceled once flourishing immersion programs.[3] Are such trips truly expressions of postmodern colonialism, as has been argued?

Geographer David Harvey, describing one of the curses of the postmodern condition, puts it this way: "Travel, even imaginary and vicarious, is supposed to broaden the mind, but it just as frequently ends up confirming prejudices."[4] Theologians Susan Thistlethwaite and George Cairns have warned of the dangers of "theological tourism."[5] Having taught numerous immersion courses myself (in various contexts in England, Germany, Zimbabwe, South Africa, Brazil, and along the US-Mexico borderlands) and having participated in a few short-term mission trips as well, I have experienced firsthand what these authors are talking about, and I share their frustration.

Perhaps the biggest problem with theological immersion experiences and short-term mission trips is that the travelers mean well and seek to learn and help but lack even a rudimentary awareness of the tremendous power differentials in which such travels take place. Such power differentials shape our relationships, yet they frequently go unnoticed. When prompted about the question of power, a colleague of mine happily reported upon her return from a faculty immersion in Latin America that there were no power differentials worth mentioning, since the North Americans got along very well with their Argentinean colleagues.

The problem is that those who find themselves on the side of power and who benefit from it are rarely aware of that fact. Matters are made worse because most religious leaders and their theologians have never been trained to analyze power even at home. In addition, while most religious travelers mean well and do not wield their power intentionally, there is also the possibility that not all travelers do mean well. I will never forget the theology student who talked to me about his pending plans to do ministry in Central America, planning to put these power differentials to good use. This student boasted about all the advantages of living in a place where he and his family could afford to have a cook, a maid and a nanny.

In a recent report, a short-term mission trip organized by some Texas churches was praised because it helped those in power to be more empathic toward poor people, noting that "people in power can become desensitized to extreme poverty." Anticipating that readers might wonder why becoming sensitized was even desirable, the report concluded, "Those in power become aware that extreme poverty is not the will of our Savior."[6] What is lacking in this well-meaning effort to develop sympathy for others is an awareness of power and of power differentials. Power appears to be a given—the report mentions people in power—but there is no question of whether extreme power differentials, in addition to extreme poverty, are contrary to the will of Christ.

What the above report also overlooks is the fact that those of us who travel on mission trips or theological immersions may not necessarily be the ones who hold the reins of power back home. The real winners of the current global situation are thus never even mentioned. Let's not forget those elite few whose fortunes continue to grow even in times of economic crisis and who have the power and the wealth to determine the future of global politics and religion. Even when power is mentioned on occasion, the real problems continue to stay invisible.

These cases are not just the problems of short-term mission trips and immersions. They mirror the stories of many missionaries around the globe who through the years honestly sought to preach the gospel of Jesus Christ and who sacrificed much to help other people, but who nevertheless unknowingly supported colonial structures. It did not matter that these missionaries meant well and that they themselves rarely benefited from the spoils of colonialism: their lack of understanding of the powers they unknowingly represented turned them into agents of colonialism. Becoming sensitive to the wisdom of those whom they sought to missionize might have led to different results.[7] Today, many people of faith, college and seminary students, and even their professors, are in the same boat. They do not benefit all that much from serving as the representatives of power either—their shares in global capital are relatively insignificant and their benefits can easily be taken away—yet they uphold the powers that be without even being aware of it.

The truth is that it never enters the mind of many religious travelers that they are connected to powers that might be harmful to those they encounter on their trips. For instance, most short-term missionaries to Russia after the end of state Communism had no idea that their travels helped set the stage for a blatant winner-take-all capitalism that was considered as American as the religion being introduced. Similarly, only very few missionaries in nineteenth-century Latin America were aware of how opening schools was crucial for North American business interests and how these schools were a prerequisite for the creation of new infrastructure and opening of new factories. In both examples, only small groups benefited from religious travel while the majority of people were worse off than before.

In such situations, merely becoming more empathic and concerned for the other is not enough. This is where I was forced to
change my own mind over the years. I once had high hopes that
developing more empathy for others would help us deal with the
sorts of problems in which religious tourism often gets caught up.
Unfortunately, there is always the possibility that the empathic
person will turn around and say, "I wish them well, but thank God
it's not me. Let me count my blessings and go back to the world of
real ministry in my own church at home." The truth is that becoming
more empathic is frequently part of tourism. In the words of theologian Susan Thistlethwaite, "Tourism depends on the appeal of the
exotic other who is different enough to titillate, while not so different that one's sense of being a 'hardened self' is threatened."[8] Such
a hardened self is unable to learn much on the road, even if it feels
that travelers and hosts are friendly and get along very well.

It might be argued, of course, that religious tourists who come
to help others do less damage than those who come to conquer,
exploit and make a profit. Yet the two movements are not so easily
separated. In the sixteenth and seventeenth centuries, Christian
missionaries and soldiers often traveled together, converting native
people if necessary by force. In the nineteenth century, Christian
educators and businesspeople traveled together, educating native
people for the workforce in the new centers of production. Today,
Christians who travel in order to help others may not realize that
they travel on the same airplanes as those who make enormous
profits from low-paid workers abroad, the same people for whom
the Christian travelers are about to build cinderblock homes or
provide free healthcare.

Most religious travelers are blissfully unaware of these differences
because the two groups stay neatly separated. While they may share
the same means of transportation and the same destination, one
group usually flies economy class, while the other flies business or

first class. Once arrived at their destination, the groups stay in entirely different neighborhoods. Those who travel in order to understand others better, and who perhaps even make an effort to learn their languages in the process, often do not realize how quickly this knowledge becomes another steppingstone for the kinds of international businesses that increase the wealth of a few without serving the interests of the majority of the people. Where is God found in all of this?

THE PROMISE OF SHORT-TERM MISSION TRIPS AND IMMERSIONS

How can religious travel be envisioned differently in this context? Thistlethwaite makes an important suggestion in this regard. She cautions that "it is not possible to think your way into other people's social conditions, you have to go there and you have to be there."[9] First steps have to be taken slowly and carefully, and a lot of patience is required. This may well be one of the hardest lessons to learn for those religious travelers who invest substantial amounts of money and effort in traveling long distances and who often have little time to stay due to a limited number of days off work. I have often observed students getting frustrated when they try to engage in conversations with others, whether on personal, political or religious issues, if there is no immediate response at a deeper level. What they tend to forget is that trust is not a privilege that a traveler can take for granted. Trust has to be earned.

While there is usually too little time to earn a deeper level of trust on an immersion or short-term mission trip, travelers' trustworthiness depends to a substantial degree on their trustworthiness developed at home. Have these travelers ever noticed the problems at home that they seek to critique and remedy abroad? Have they ever addressed them at home? Have these travelers ever dealt with issues of power along the lines of race, class and gender before leaving on short-term mission and immersion trips? Have they ever taken a stand with those who occupy less-privileged positions at home? In order to prepare for immersion and short-term mission trips, travelers would do well to begin paying attention at home before they leave, so that they can pay closer attention on the road. Matters will continue to develop from there. What they will be able to see after they return home is likely to surprise them.

To be sure, the track record of the institution the travelers represent also plays a role. While individual travelers may never have visited the destinations to which they travel, their institutions have histories of engagements that precede individuals and to which they contribute in turn. And let us not forget the track record of our countries. This is where Americans may have to work harder than many others today, due to the history of US global involvement in the past decades. Many Americans are not aware how deeply our country has been involved in many places abroad; currently, the United States military alone is involved in over 150 countries around the world and US businesses span the globe, for better or for worse.

In my travels, I have found that it is often easier to talk about critical issues that concern people when I tell them I am German than when I tell them I am a US citizen, although I never try to hide the fact that I live and work in the United States. Unfortunately, many people around the globe are unaware that there are alternative voices in the United States and that not all of its citizens benefit from or agree with official policies, business practices or what is often perceived as dominant US religion. At this point, wonderful opportunities offer themselves to religious travelers from the United States to talk about these alternative voices and the many people's movements that have shaped US history for the better, like the Civil Rights movement, the suffragists' and women's movements, the Chicano movement, and old and new religion and labor movements. Religious travelers telling these stories should never forget to mention that all of these movements have religious components. It may well be that in the process of telling this often-neglected side of US history, religious travelers learn something about their own histories as well!

Another way to support the process of forming trust is by including younger people in the group. When I took my children along on immersion trips with theology students—against the policy of my school, which implied that bringing children along on academic trips was a distraction—many people we visited appeared to be more open to us. My children's questions were often answered with great care and sincerity, initiating deeper levels of trust and creating openings for other questions by the group. I will always remember the time we took a group of theology students from the United States and our nine-year-old twin daughters to a newly formed settlement of the Landless Movement (MST) outside of São Paulo, Brazil. When travelers and hosts saw that the children intuitively felt at ease, the encounters and conversations began to flow better and in more relaxed fashion, despite the very real pressures of the situation, which included the constant threat of violence against the movement. Traveling with children also had a major influence on the travelers themselves, particularly on those who had never traveled to places in the Global South.

I have often seen students and fellow religious travelers disappointed because their hosts would not open up and tell them their whole life story in the first five minutes of an encounter. Understanding power differentials helps us develop a sense for why this is so and why it might be a good thing. In a situation where grave differentials of power exist, open encounters cannot be expected and should not be demanded, as they would leave those with less power even more vulnerable than they already are. This is an important lesson especially for the leaders of immersion and mission groups who would like to speed things up and produce lasting experiences for the group. Yet just as earning trust takes time, truly listening to others takes time and care as well. And even when we have listened long and hard, leaders of immersion and mission groups should never assume there is a point when we know enough or that the other has finished speaking.[10]

A colleague and friend of mine from the United States who often traveled to Latin America refused to teach theology classes there for several years because he truly wanted to take time to listen to the people. This is commendable, as too many of us fail to take enough time to listen. Unfortunately, the moment when one has listened enough, enabling one to teach (or preach) elsewhere in the same way one would at home, may never come. A better way to deal with this problem might be to teach not by telling others what they need to know and do but how we are dealing with our own problems at home. This approach, which has served me well over the years, invites others to compare their problems to our problems. This means, of course, that I am not in control. Neither can I claim that what I have to teach must all be relevant elsewhere in exactly the same way: those who listen to my presentations are the ones who decide what matters in their context, and it is only in the subsequent discussions and conversations that we can discuss relevant material.

All of this points to a fundamental paradigm change in our relationship to God: if we realize we are not in control, we can begin to learn and deepen our own experiences of the struggles of life.

ENDURING THE SHOCK OF DIFFERENCE

While short-term mission trips and immersion experiences will always be skewed due to power differentials produced by those with economic, political, cultural and religious dominance, there is hope. Although openness and empathy are not enough, travelers can still expect to engage in genuine learning processes and broaden their horizons. Of course, in order to do this, they will have to learn how to endure what might be called the "shock of difference," which comes in various shapes and forms. Travelers have an opportunity to learn not merely that "other people are just like us," as enlightened people often tell their children. While understanding that others are not less human than us is important, saying that "they are like us" means we still use ourselves as the norm. Even saying that "we are all the same" does not quite move quite far enough.

Travelers who move out of their personal safety zone can take one more step and learn that "we are like other people." We are no longer the norm for humanity, no matter how benevolent and well-meaning we think we are. Breaking through our self-centeredness helps us become open to being challenged by others and to become more fully human, as well as more fully Christian, together. The proof of what was learned on the journey will be seen when we return home, and this needs to be assessed carefully and over the long term. Such a journey will not end after we return home but continue to move us.

In search of better models for religious travels, we can learn from the insights of what has been called "toxic tourism." This term refers to organized tours of environmental devastation and poisoning in underprivileged communities in the United States, which are much more likely to be chosen for the location of dumps, heavy industry and other activities that endanger the environment. "Environmental racism" is another term that describes these kinds of problems, which are widespread. Toxic tourists are aware that in their travels they are encountering life-and-death matters in more pressing forms than they encounter in their own neighborhoods. It is precisely this awareness that religious tourists need to develop as well.

The first step in this model is to understand the challenges that modern mass tourism poses, with the goal of developing more constructive ways of travel. As communications scholar Phaedra Pezzullo has noted, "By definition tourists are invasive and ignorant of their surroundings. Tourists make waste, take resources, destroy—or, at minimum transform—places, and encourage local communities literally to sell themselves and to commodify their culture for money." This view from an ecological perspective puts in sharper relief many of the insights we have developed in this chapter. Using toxicity as a metaphor exposes the problems of tourism in acidic language: *"Tourism is toxic.* Tourism contaminates the people and the places where it occurs. Tourism corrodes. Tourism offends. Tourism exploits. In a sense, some might even conclude, tourism kills."[11] Religious tourism, as we have seen, can have its own corrosive effects.

How hard is it for a camel to go through the eye of a needle? Is there any way tourism can be redeemed? Pezzullo's toxic tourism encourages us to pay attention to situations "when practices of tourism may be motivated by our more admirable desires for fun, connection, difference, civic spirit, social and environmental change, and education."[12] When seen from this angle, immersion and short-term mission trips point in the right direction, because most travelers share a positive motivation. On this basis the self-critical work can begin. On toxic tours, "tourists are asked to expose themselves to the costs of human greed: poisoned air, polluted water, degraded land, and bodies that are diseased, deformed, or dying."[13] This is an important component for more productive immersion and short-term mission trips as well. What if, like toxic tourists, we were to expose ourselves intentionally to the costs of human greed, paying attention not so much to examples of individual greed but to the institutional greed that is part and parcel of the economics of capitalism?

On the immersion trips I have led, this question is a constant component. Encounters with immigrants at the US-Mexico border, for instance, have taught us that people migrate for life-and-death reasons; they are not able to make a living back home because global capitalism does not value their resources, either their land or their labor. Members of the Landless Movement in Brazil have reminded us of the difficulties homeless people face when they want to survive and work for a living, as their efforts to occupy unused portions of land in order to grow food are often met with deadly violence by the landowners. Inhabitants of the townships in South Africa have provided us with living proof that after the end of racial apartheid, there is no end in sight to what might be called economic apartheid, as the rich grow richer and the poor grow poorer.

All these examples touch the deepest nerves of life, as we are confronted with real death and dying. But perhaps for me it was a gang-related shooting outside a Methodist church in Rio de Janeiro, where I traveled a few years ago for some presentations without bringing a group, that brought home most forcefully the life-and-death tensions in which we find ourselves. These tensions reflect and mimic the broader tensions produced by global capitalism, where tens of thousands die every day from preventable causes like hunger and disease. When one's own life is in danger, one learns unforgettable lessons. This experience brought back memories of a death threat I received during the early days of my teaching at Perkins School of Theology at Southern Methodist University. Back then, a few colleagues and I received letters from a racist supremacist group telling us they would get rid of us if we kept doing what we were doing. I do not wish such experiences on anyone, but my life was changed forever through them. There was no going back.

What we learn in these situations, of course, is not all negative and depressing. Among the most amazing experiences of immersion travel is the realization that people are not giving up despite being confronted with death and that they are producing life-giving alternatives instead. When I returned to the above-mentioned settlement of the Brazilian Landless Movement six years after I had first visited it, the people had built modest houses and were selling their self-grown produce. They had even learned to grow and produce wine. But much more important than their ability to take part in the economy was that they had succeeded in permanently winning the use of the land that would otherwise have gone unused, as settlements of the Landless Movements gained legal status after a certain amount of time. And they had succeeded in forming a lasting community of resistance.

Unlike the students who travel with me to Africa or Latin America, students who go with me to Europe often expect a smooth ride, with visits to sites of the past glory of Christianity. Yet these students experience their own shock of difference when they are not artificially sheltered from what is happening on the ground. By the same token, there are too many travels to countries south of the equator where such a shock of difference is not experienced because the travelers remain in their bubbles.

Students who travel to Europe experience the shock of difference and learn something about themselves when confronted with the histories of European empire and fascism. Surprisingly small numbers of students have considered that imprisoning people without warrants and fair trials, and holding them indefinitely, did not happen only in German concentration camps but also is part of US history and today is still going on in the prison camps of Guantánamo Bay. Neither are they aware that for Germans the idea of a national flag in a church sanctuary is a sensitive issue, as it was German fascism that started the practice.

When immersion travelers become aware of the toxicity of their own environments in firsthand encounters with others, they are invariably shocked. Yet it is in the midst of those shocks that a deeper solidarity becomes possible and that travel develops the potential to transform. This kind of solidarity keeps broadening. It includes not just the travelers and their hosts but also encompasses the relationships among the travelers themselves and drives awareness of those back home whom religious people need to take more seriously: immigrants, the homeless, those suffering from economic injustice, and those who are the victims of what one of our German guides, Jürgen Hestler, calls "everyday fascism": people of oppressed racial, political, gender and sexual orientations.[14]

Finding God in these shocks of difference makes all the difference in the world.

THE URBAN MINISTRY ALTERNATIVE

Another model for more constructive travels by religious people can be developed from what has become known in Christian circles as "urban ministry," which constitutes a form of travel within the city that can be just as enlightening as long-distance travel. This sort of ministry confronts us with the paradox that "people travel to faraway places to watch, in fascination, the kind of people they ignore at home."[15] Urban ministry thus encourages churches to counter their self-centeredness and their narcissism, get out of their pews and other static locations, and travel to the parts of their own towns that they usually bypass and ignore.

There are two very different theological models of urban ministry, which resemble two very different approaches to religious travel. Both models agree that urban ministry seeks to address the mission of the church in the world, which is ultimately God's own mission. Both further agree that urban ministry needs to deal with the fact that most mainline churches have traveled out of the inner cities during the past forty years, following white flight and a general trend of escape to the suburbs. What happens as churches begin to travel in the other direction, trying to find their way back into the cities?

The default theological model of urban ministry, which is mostly implicit but for this reason all the more widespread, is built on the assumption that the church's task is to bring God back into the cities. The theological model further assumes that God left the cities when the churches left and moved to the suburbs with them.

Mission, in this context, means to proclaim in the cities the God whose home base is the buildings of suburban churches. Religious travel often follows this model as well, as the travelers assume they are proclaiming in other parts of the world the God who is located in their home countries and home churches. And while religious travelers are for the most part open to acknowledging the presence of God elsewhere, especially in more "primitive" contexts, they measure this God by the standards of their own God. It does not occur to them that their God might need to be measured by the standards of the God who is at work in the world and whom they thus encounter in their travels.

An alternative theological model of urban ministry—one that is just as applicable to short-term mission trips—starts with the assumption that God did not leave the cities when the churches left. Following this model, the task of the churches is fundamentally different. Not only are the churches not carrying God back into the cities; the churches need to return to the cities in order to find God at work there and to understand the reality of God more fully. Unless they look for God where God is at work, they may miss the reality of God altogether.

Ministry and mission in this context are not determined by the church but by God, who is at work inside *and* outside the church and in communities that the churches hardly ever notice. This theological model provides a new horizon for religious travelers. One of the key reasons for travel according to this model is to observe God at work elsewhere, in other places and communities, and to join God and others in this work. This broadening of horizons is important not because it gives the travelers more theological options but because it challenges some of the travelers' most cherished images of God. I have seen this happen when students told me after immersions in West Dallas that meeting God there changed their lives.

Of course, not everyone is open to this, and religious travelers should be prepared for pushback. While many institutions support immersion experiences today, not all of them are equally interested in learning the hard lessons that come in these contexts.

GOING WHERE GOD IS AT WORK

German theologian Dietrich Bonhoeffer understood that if we truly want to find God, we have to look for God where God has preceded us.[16] If we look for God without following God, our images of God will not only be limited; they will be so distorted that we miss the reality of God altogether. Bonhoeffer and many other theologians have argued that God has preceded us into the places of tension and trouble in this world, into the toxic places and the places on the underside of history, where the churches often dare not go. From a prison cell in Hitler's Germany Bonhoeffer notes that it is "an experience of incomparable value" that he has learned "to see the great events of world history from below, from the perspective of the outcast, the suspects, the maltreated, the powerless, the oppressed, the reviled—in short, from the perspective of those who suffer."[17] If following God into these places is not optional, religious travel may not be optional either. Here everything changes.

The good news is that such fresh encounters with God and with other people do happen on immersion and mission trips. No matter how privileged the travelers and how regulated and structured the trip, these things cannot be controlled. Unfortunately, many of our standard models of theology and ministry are not able to deal with such encounters, so their challenge shrivels up and is lost after people return to their "normal" religious settings. Pushing beyond the sort of religious tourism that only reinforces religious narcissism requires new relationships with the world, with other people and with the divine Other. In a nutshell, alternative travel is a matter of forming new relationships that allow for two-way com-

munication and are open-ended. Here lies the ultimate challenge
for the religious travelers, because forming new relationships is not
possible unless we acknowledge and deal with the often-distorted
relationships already in place—relationships produced by long colonial histories as well as by contemporary structures of cultural
dominance and economic exploitation.

The primary reason so many immersion and short-mission trips
fall short or even fail is not that people do not mean well. The
failure has often to do with meaning too well. Meaning well and
wanting to see the other as equal, we often fail to give an account
of the deeper inequalities produced by power differentials. Unless
we understand who we are and become aware of these inequalities,
we are not in a position where we can learn from the other.

One of the common models of helping others displays the
problem. "Give a man a fish and you feed him for a day; teach a man
to fish and you feed him for a lifetime"—so the old saying goes.
What is not acknowledged here, however, is the asymmetry of
power that does not allow us to understand the real reasons people
do not have fish. What if their lakes have been fished empty by
commercial fleets? What if their waters have been contaminated by
heavy industry? What if someone has built a fence around the lake?
What if their lakes have been dried up because of extensive water
use upstream? In none of these cases is the problem that people do
not know how to fish. The problem is the lack of access to fish because of a differential of power.

A lack of the awareness of the asymmetry of power is also behind
much empowerment talk. Assuming that those of us who have some
power can pass it on to people who lack it is naive at several levels: it
fails to ask what it is that disempowers people in the first place and
what to do about it, and it assumes too quickly that middle-class
church people in America or Europe have much power to make a
difference. As travelers, we might be able to overcome this naivety as

we learn what it really takes to make a difference. One thing is for sure: we will not make a difference without forming relationships and without investigating where God is truly at work.

The biggest challenge of immersion and short-term mission trips, which is also the biggest promise, is that we are led to take a deeper look at ourselves. Mission in particular begins not, as is often assumed, with the conversion of other people by the missionary. Mission begins with the conversion of the self of the missionary in light of God's mission. Before we can become part of any sort of solution, we need to develop a sense of how we have come to be (and still are) part of the problem. This is the story of the disciples of Jesus. When Peter encounters Jesus, before he can join the movement, he makes this confession: "Go away from me, Lord, for I am a sinful man!" (Lk 5:8).

Immersion and short-term mission trips become truly alternative ways of travel when they lead us to take an extended and deep look at ourselves and at our interconnectedness with others and with God. This includes an awareness of how others are related inversely to us and our collective identities in a globalizing world. In this light, the biggest challenge of all may well be coming home. Yet this is also where the greatest promise lies.

five

Travel as an Act of Justice

In *Travel as Political Act,* well-known travel journalist Rick Steves discusses some of the political underpinnings of travel. He rightly argues that travel can help Americans develop a better understanding of the interconnectedness of the contemporary world and of their own place in it. Broadening people's horizons leads to acts of resistance against narrow-mindedness and bigotry, which are widespread. Traveling with Steves has the potential to open people's eyes, and his travel reports are aimed at this goal as well. Steves even deals with some of the more challenging questions that American travelers are bound to encounter on the road, like whether America is an empire or not. His response to this question is insightful, as he points out that our opinions on this topic hardly matter when the world sees us that way.

Nevertheless, while travel is indeed a political act, there is more to it than Steves realizes. Many of his analyses stay safely on the surface. His take on the American empire is a case in point. It is one thing to challenge the hard power of empire, which is not difficult to see in the use of violence and military might that seeks to control others without the hard work of building relationships. But what about other, softer powers that empires use to establish their dominance? While awareness of hard power is a start, without taking a look at the soft powers of empire, we cannot engage in travel as an act of justice in our time.

It is striking that Steves sees no problem with soft power: "If we can soften the way we wield our power," he concludes, "we might find some solutions that work better for us . . . and for the rest of the planet."[1] What Steves does not tell us is that softened forms of power are not new, as they have been used by empires for thousands of years. The Roman Empire did not expand merely by force but also by integrating people into its structures and by providing people certain limited privileges in order to appease them. Today, we can consider the economic structural adjustment policies imposed on the poor that drive migrants from their homes, as well as the global advertising industry that shapes people's tastes and desires for the benefit of large corporations. Here is where those of us intent on traveling for the purposes of justice need to take a closer look.

As we have seen, the soft powers of empire are even embedded to a certain degree in tourism, including the travels of religious tourists and pilgrims. Soft power in its own way reinforces the crass asymmetries that mark our times as the rich get richer and the poor get poorer. To be sure, soft power is nothing new. It has been the primary mode of expansion of colonialism and neocolonialism since the eighteenth and nineteenth centuries.[2]

Various experiences on the road can help us sharpen our notion of travel as an act of justice. Just as travel can contribute to a better understanding of the power differentials in the worlds of politics and economics, it can help Christians develop a deeper sense of the power differentials in global Christianity and what to do about them. From their earliest beginnings, the Jewish-Christian traditions found themselves in the force fields of great empires, and these empires had to be negotiated in light of a God who would rather remain on the road indefinitely than settle for the dominant status quo. Isn't that also the story of Jesus of Nazareth? "Foxes have holes, and birds of the air have nests; but the Son of Man has nowhere to lay his head" (Lk 9:58).

Of course, other traditions within Judaism and Christianity sought to confine this divine movement by building temples and shrines where God would be located and attempting to tie God to one place alone. The prophet Amos speaks for many others when he has God challenge the established places of worship and invite the people to keep mobile:

> Seek me and live;
>> but do not seek Bethel,
> and do not enter into Gilgal
>> or cross over to Beer-sheba;
> for Gilgal shall surely go into exile,
>> and Bethel shall come to nothing. (Amos 5:4-5)

Just as travel can turn into an act of justice, so can religion when it takes shape on the road.

TRAVEL'S INFLUENCE ON MODERN THEOLOGY

A brief consideration of how travel has shaped modern theology will help us understand the promises and pitfalls with which we are faced today and why travel as an act of justice might be more important now than ever. Modern theology was born in the eighteenth and nineteenth centuries in a world that had become more mobile than ever before, during the time of the great exploratory travels that broadened the horizons of Europe and the United States and expanded their fortunes. These exploratory travels sparked great popular interest. Travel writing was in vogue, and people devoured the books that were published. Even Prussian theologian Friedrich Schleiermacher, widely recognized as the father of modern theology, felt compelled to contribute. Although he never traveled abroad himself, he put together four volumes on the history of the settlement of Australia.[3] As most of these volumes have been lost, none of this would be worth mentioning today if it did not also help us understand the core issues that shaped modern theology and much of the tradition on which the contemporary church stands.

In the eighteenth and nineteenth centuries, the popular fascination with travel to exotic places and with the people encountered there was tied to a basic appreciation of the world and other people. European readers wanted to become acquainted with what was going on elsewhere and to gain a broader understanding of the world in which they lived. This appreciation for people and for the world led to major changes in theological thinking. In Schleiermacher's theology, encounters with people on the road were envisioned in terms of attraction rather than coercion.[4] The Spanish conquest, along with the hard power and coercive qualities it embodied, was now declared a thing of the past. The hard power of the sixteenth century was judged negatively. Soft power, as embodied by enlightened northern European colonialism, was declared the way of the future. More specifically, German-speaking people envisioned civilizing missions, believing that the business interests of other northern European countries were still harmful.

Christ himself, Schleiermacher proposed, never coerced people but worked exclusively through the powers of attraction. Moreover, if the church had sought to expand through attraction instead of trying to coerce people to adopt Christianity, he claimed, the whole world would have become Christian by his time. The modern interest in hermeneutics—the art of interpretation—had its origins here, as people in Europe began to think about how to communicate with others in noncoercive ways. Fresh encounters with others by exploratory travelers led to real efforts to understand them, including their languages, traditions and religions. This is the beginning not only of the modern study of religion but also of academic fields such as anthropology and sociology. The roots of developmental aid can be found here as well.

HARD AND SOFT POWER

Nevertheless, while these encounters with others through exploratory travels were an improvement over earlier travels for the sake of conquest, they were limited in many ways. As hard power was rejected and soft power moved into its place, power became more difficult to see and to analyze. One key reason Western scholars of religion could be so generous to others and develop new appreciation for other religions was that they never doubted their cultural, political and economic superiority. The colonial power differentials between those who saw themselves as civilized and those who were considered "primitive" backed them up. This was the case even if, like the Prussians in Schleiermacher's time, they did not have their own colonies and benefited only indirectly from the colonies of other European nations.

It was, of course, these colonial powers and interests that made travel and exploration possible in the first place. Colonial interests explored the travel routes and secured them, providing means of transportation and an infrastructure. When things were stabilized abroad in this way, the powers of attraction could be relied upon. On these foundations developed a sincere trust that the higher and more powerful entities would not only attract but ultimately also assimilate the lower ones. Even the modern theological appreciation for other religions needs to be seen in this context. While they broadened their horizons so as to include other religions in their study of religion, Schleiermacher and many others presupposed the superiority of their own Christianity, of the Protestant and European variety, and developed complex taxonomies categorizing various religions as more and less advanced. Even those who dedicated their lives to studying other religions with appreciation, like the German Sanskrit scholar Friedrich Max Müller, who worked in England, did so in order to revitalize the best qualities of Christianity at home.[5] The theological, cultural and political are thus always closely related.

The history of tourism continues these trajectories. Dean Mac-Cannell has argued that mainline tourism produces new cultural forms on a global base, and I would argue that religion follows similar dynamics:

> In the name of tourism, capital and modernized peoples have been deployed to the most remote regions of the world, farther than any army was ever sent. Institutions have been established to support this deployment, not just hotels, restaurants, and transportation systems, but restorations of ancient shrines, development of local handicrafts for sale to tourists, and rituals performed for tourists. In short, tourism is not just an aggregate of merely commercial activities; it is also an ideological framing of history, nature, and tradition; a framing that has the power to reshape culture and nature to its own ends.[6]

As we have seen in previous chapters, pilgrimage, vagabonding and religious tourism have made their own contributions to spreading the interests of Western modernity and global capitalism, as have certain forms of immersion and short-term mission trips. If these efforts to colonize not only politics and economics but also culture, nature and even religion are indeed part of our heritage, there is no escaping the urgent need for alternative experiences of travel as theological and political acts of justice.

The Hilton representative cited earlier, who claimed that "each of our hotels is a little America," knows what is at stake when he adds that "we are doing our bit to spread world peace, and to fight socialism."[7] What is not said explicitly here, of course, is that this sort of tourism also helps to spread global capitalism and the severe and growing power differentials between the rich and the poor. Along the same lines, it has often been argued that tourism makes important contributions to economic development. Between 1969 and 1979, the World Bank maintained a department of tourism. While this department was abandoned due to criticism, the World Bank has remained very active in the promotion of tourism for the sake of development.[8] The goal of these efforts is to deregulate and liberalize the tourism sector in order to increase the profitability of tourism in the developing world, which is, of course, where the highest rates of growth are achieved.[9]

When tourists and locals encounter one another, discrepancies in wealth and power always play a role, whether consciously or unconsciously. These discrepancies mirror the broader differentials of power at home between the privileged, who may not always be conscious of their privilege, and the rest, who are often only too painfully aware of their lack of privilege. In the context of traveling, discrepancies in wealth and power are exacerbated not only between tourists and locals but also among the locals themselves. On a visit to Peru, my wife and I took a Peruvian seminary student from a modest background to a little restaurant for some hamburgers. Upon the student's request for some "salsa," the waiter left no doubt about the superiority of the product his restaurant offered, noting that the sauce was no mere salsa; it was ketchup. ("No es salsa, es ketchup.")

No global-resistance movement yet has engaged tourism the way resistance movements have engaged the World Trade Organization or Wall Street; resistance is usually more localized. Nevertheless, tourism is increasingly seen in a critical perspective and alternative forms of travel are being explored. At a global summit on tourism, questions were raised as to who benefits from tourism. Equally important, demands were made to democratize tourism. The search, it was announced, is on for a tourism that is "'pro people' and based on justice."[10]

MAKING TRAVEL A FORM OF JUSTICE

Travel as a theological and political act of justice pushes us beyond our colonial and neocolonial heritage and beyond the asymmetries of both hard and soft power. The most important lesson to be learned here is that travel never occurs in a vacuum. Responsible travel needs to take into account the power structures that frame individual travel experiences. To those who travel on the side of privilege, attention to power structures may seem optional—this is still the case for many traveling religious groups. Migrants and others who travel in far less privileged contexts can teach us a lesson in this regard; their survival may depend on being aware of these power structures. Travel as a theological and political act of justice brings together these various experiences and helps us realize the sort of interconnectedness that benefits the wealthy and the powerful, with the goal of developing a new sort of global interconnectedness that benefits everyone.

Perhaps the simplest way travel is connected to justice is found in its inherent disruptive quality. Even travel that is integrated into people's lives, taking place during vacations and officially sanctioned downtime, implies some letting go and quitting, if only in a very mild sense. The simple act of locking up one's apartment or house and leaving behind a garden, pets and friends is meaningful in this regard. While letting go and quitting does not come easy for those of us who strongly identify with our work or our home, we find here the first steps toward a more just ordering of things. Small steps matter. I will never forget the surprise of one of my professors in graduate school when I mentioned to him that my wife, our dog and I were planning to travel across the United States in an old VW van one summer, without particular research plans. I still remember his disapproval as we took off one weekend to Cusco, Peru, in order to see Machu Picchu when we were doing research in Lima, Peru.

The power of the act of quitting should not be underestimated. Even those who travel merely to escape the everyday can learn to identify with the disruptive qualities of travel. What is disrupted are the structures of dominant power and the rules created to hold us down. Perhaps the motto of *memento mori* (remember that you have to die), which once upon a time pushed pilgrims out on the road in search for eternal life, could be interpreted slightly differently here: "do not forget to die." Dying to the expectations of the status quo is a powerful thing.

Religion scholar Frederick Ruf has identified a religious moment in travel that is often overlooked: "What travel means is not just misfortune but seeking misfortune. In some sense, wanting it. And it is of such crucial importance to us that we must call it religious. Leaving home, stepping into the way that will lead us away, far away, walking among strangers, being stunned, getting lost—those are religious behaviors."[11] What Ruf describes here is the disruptive quality of travel, although less fortunate travelers would remind us that we should be careful what we wish for. The rather superficial "love of ruptures" celebrated by Ruf endangers the search for justice to some degree.

Ruf recalls not only the shock of observing a woman without hands and feet trying to eat in a public place in India, but also of traveling with his teenage children in Jamaica and staying in a midrange hotel outside of a resort, wondering what kind of a parent would "dis-locate his children like this."[12] No doubt something can be learned from such experiences, but the notions of "rupture" and "seeking misfortune" are hardly appropriate here. True rupture and misfortune is like the judgment of God: while it may be necessary for the transformation of the world, it is not the sort of thing that can be enjoyed.

SOME CONCLUDING THEOLOGICAL REFLECTIONS ON JUSTICE

The understanding of justice that is emerging from these reflections on traveling is closely related to the understanding of justice found in the Bible. In many biblical texts, justice refers to the covenant—in other words, to a relationship between God and humanity that is dynamic and responsive. This relationship is expressed in terms of God's faithfulness, which implies God's special concern for those pushed to the margins of the covenant and excluded by some who are under the mistaken impression that they are closer to God.[13] Justice has to do therefore with a particular concern for the restoration of relationship with those on the margins, such as the widows, orphans and strangers of the Old Testament and the fishermen, prostitutes and tax collectors of the New Testament. More specifically, in the prophets of the Old Testament, the term "justice" addresses the distorted relationships between the rich and the poor caused by oppressive actions of the rich who "trample on the poor" (Amos 5:11).[14]

In this context, establishing and restoring relationship with people pushed to the margins is not simply a social issue or the moral consequence of faith. Much more is at stake—the quality of our relationship to God is connected to this matter as well. Distortions in our relations to others get reproduced in distortions in our relations to God and vice versa. Justice as establishing new relationships with those who experience injustice and who are excluded from the covenant makes a difference in several ways.

First, such justice is linked to detailed accounts of the kinds of pressures that people on the margins have to endure in their lives and in which travelers to a certain extent share. Here a sharper understanding of the dangers and injustices of empires emerges since people on the margins and on the road experience them in their own bodies, much more directly than anyone else. Viewing life from the perspective of those pushed to the margins, there can be no illusion of equality or a level playing field, resulting in a structural understanding of injustice.

One example of such a structural understanding of injustice relates to a reassessment of individualism. Does individualism really exist or is it the myth of the powerful? Is the wealth of corporate America built singlehandedly by a few prominent CEOs, as their compensation seems to indicate, or is it rather tied to the labor of billions around the globe who work under constantly worsening conditions? The challenge is thus different from what is usually envisioned. It is not to become "less individualistic" but to become aware of the relationships already in place, to put an end to the cover-up, and to form relationships that are less asymmetric and more dynamic and responsive. This insight has important implications for our relationship to God as well.

Second, justice has to do with the restoration of relationships, including those of victim and offender. The so-called preferential option for the poor of Latin American liberation theology has often been misunderstood as a special interest arrangement that destroys community by neglecting the rich. Yet this was never the intention, since the problem can obviously not be resolved without the rich. In a situation marked by severe asymmetry, invoking principles like fairness will not suffice to rectify the problem. A preferential option for the poor includes those who distort relationships and who benefit most from asymmetry—but it reminds us that they are faced with a particular challenge; they are the ones who need not only a little push but all the help they can get.

The energy that bubbles up from the margins and on the road (God's own location in Christ's ministry, death and resurrection) provides some help by pushing toward justice not in punitive or redistributive ways but in the initiation of transformed relationships. This transformation is what turns travel into acts of justice. The meaning of "love" is transformed in the process, making Jesus' commandment to love one's neighbor as oneself (Mk 12:31) appear in new light. Love of neighbor is not just another commandment but a reminder of the deeper relationships with our neighbor that are already in place. What if we read Jesus' words as "love your

neighbor as [being] yourself"? When we relate to our neighbors in
this sense, our horizons broaden as we begin to understand that we
are already connected whether we acknowledge it or not. Travelers
are in a better position to realize this than those who stay in their
own safety zones. Moreover, such a reshaped relationship with our
neighbor ("love") introduces a different note in our relationship
with God ("love the Lord"; Mk 12:30) as well.

Travel as an act of justice throws new light on our vision of God.
The biblical sources, although not lacking in differences, converge
in various important ways in their focus on relationship. The
Hebrew verb ṣdq means to be faithful to the community established
by God in the covenant.[15] The Greek term *dikaiosynē*, as used in
the New Testament, maintains this emphasis on relationship. Although there is no uniform notion of justice in the New Testament,
justice tends to include both the relationships between human
beings and the relationship to God; here is a significant difference
from the classical Greek notion of *dikaiosynē*, which focuses exclusively on the relationship between human beings.[16]

The distortion of relationships by oppression is a concern in various
parts of the Bible—the Psalms come to mind as one prominent
example—and can also be found in Jesus' message and other parts of
the New Testament. Justice in all these cases aims at the restoration of
relationships and at putting an end to oppression. The primary concern
of justice is thus not so much helping those in need but overcoming
oppressive relationships and learning how to relate differently—both
to other human beings and to God. The apostle Paul's notion of justification needs to be seen in a similar light: not simply as a religious
transaction but as a manifestation of God's justice, which resists injustice and reconstructs distorted relationship.[17] As a result, justice as
restoring broken relationships needs to address the power differential
between oppressor and oppressed and it is partisan insofar as God
sides with those who are trampled underfoot.

The image of God that emerges here is dynamic. Those who want to know God need to do so on their feet, participating in God's creative transformation of oppressive relationships. Picking up an insight from Dietrich Bonhoeffer, we might say that we need to follow God where God is preceding us. The question then is not whether "God is on our side" (a common assumption of the privileged) but whether "we are on God's side," taking sides in the dynamic pursuit of God's justice.

THEOLOGY ON THE ROAD

Travel can become an act of justice when we recognize that our encounters with others whom we meet on the road are vital both for the world and for the church, as well as for our understanding of God. In the midst of these encounters, acknowledging asymmetries and tensions, we can experience the divine in fresh ways, following 1 John 4:20: "Those who say, 'I love God,' and hate their brothers and sisters, are liars; for those who do not love a brother or sister whom they have seen, cannot love God whom they have not seen." In this context, travel puts us on the road to justice as it helps us reenvision the Christian witness and the Christian life.

The profound trouble with static theology should now be abundantly clear. Static theology that is not on the move toward encounters with other people and with the world is unable to be on the move toward encounters with God either. Those who do not recognize and positively shape their interconnectedness with others will not be able to recognize and positively shape their interconnectedness with God either. Or as I pointed out years ago, those who are not able to muster respect and love for others will hardly be able to muster respect and love for God.[18] Theology on the road is the best antidote to static, self-centered theology.

Travel brings us closer together with other people and places us in solidarity with them, forcing us to give up control. Of all the forms of travel, the travel of migrants is best able to expose the lies of the status quo that tell us things are fine and we should not worry about the direction in which the dominant powers lead us. Vagabonds and pilgrims sometimes come to similar conclusions. Jesus' question about the nature of his true family reminds us that we often find ourselves closer to fellow travelers on the road than to those who seek to uphold the status quo of empire, family and church. For those who exchange some of their privileges for being on the road, narcissism is no longer an option, whether it is the narcissism of the individual, the family, the church, the nation or of those who benefit from the global economy while billions suffer.

We take the next step in thinking about travel as an act of justice when we begin to understand that the static and universal ideas with which we have been raised are usually the tools of dominant powers. This is true in politics and economics as well as religion. Even parents sometimes embody this spirit when they tell their children, "That's the way things are." Universal definitions of how things are, how they always have been, and how they always will be are usually in the interest of those who benefit from the status quo. The empires of the past, whether Egypt, Rome or Britain, had their seemingly eternal rules (just think of the Victorian Age), and contemporary empires claim their own universals, convinced that "capitalism is here to stay" or "God blesses America." Traveling can help us expose the relative nature of such seemingly universal claims.

At the same time, traveling can also help us expose a sort of contextual theology that has become static, celebrating the seemingly unchanging context of women, the poor, African Americans, Latinos and Latinas, and LGBTQ people. Too many contextual thinkers still proceed on the basis of identity politics, which presupposes the rather fixed identities of various groups without considering the more interesting question of how these various groups are related to each other and on the move.

Contextual theology done on the road can never be static, as it exposes the networks of power in which we "live and move and have our being" (Acts 17:28). Migrant theology knows that it emerges in the tensions of capitalism that play off migrant workers and their employers; women's theology on the road knows that it emerges in the tensions of patriarchy that play off women and men; liberation theologies that shape up on the road are able to take into account the dynamics of race and class that involve not just the oppressed but also the oppressors, as they pit against each other white Americans, African Americans, Latino Americans and Asian Americans, as well as working class and ruling class. The context that matters, therefore, is never just the context that is closest to home. The contexts that matter are the contexts we encounter as we are on the road together, the contexts where we find our common pain. These are the contexts where God travels: "If one member [of the body of Christ] suffers, all suffer together with it," the apostle Paul states (1 Cor 12:26). And in the words of the Son of Man, "Just as you did it to one of the least of these who are members of my family, you did it to me" (Mt 25:40).

Doing theology on the road and engaging in acts of justice, therefore, helps us overcome the dangers of static approaches and the commodification of particular locations and issues, which usually happens in service of the status quo. Proprietary theology is no longer an option. Yet not just any kind of movement and travel will do. In the Sermon on the Mount, Jesus talks about the easy and the hard roads: "Enter through the narrow gate; for the gate is wide and the road is easy that leads to destruction, and there are many who take it. For the gate is narrow and the road is hard that leads to life, and there are few who find it" (Mt 7:13-14). John Wesley, in his comment on the passage, puts things bluntly in a question to his audience: "Are there many wise, many rich, many mighty or noble, travelling with you in the same way? By this token, without going any farther, you know it does not lead to life."[19] There is something that those who travel on the easy roads of this world miss—the sort of things that well-to-do travelers, mass tourists and even the religious travelers of the status quo miss: the life that is not destructive of self and others and, by extension, an encounter with the life of God.

An insight by a traveler who experienced the hard times and displacements of the Thirty Years' War of the sixteenth century, one of the most devastating wars in Europe, helps us deepen our understanding of travel as political and theological act of justice. In one of his famous epigrams, Friedrich von Logau states that in situations of danger and great need, the middle road leads to death. Those who travel in the comfort of the wealthy and the powerful are not the only ones who miss what is most important. Those who seek to keep safely in the middle also are in trouble.

To understand the reasons for this, one needs to understand the flow of power. Lacking the courage to take sides, those who seek the deceiving balance of the middle road are invariably pulled toward the greater force field, often without even being aware of it. This is a problem for tourists, religious travelers, pilgrims, vagabonds and even some migrants. Without taking the sides of those with whom the God of the Jewish-Christian traditions of the road tends to side—the slaves, exiles, widows, orphans, strangers, fishermen, shepherds, refugees and dissidents of the various empires—travelers will not be able to establish just relationships. Like the dominant roads of the elites, the middle roads lead to death and destruction.

What is the alternative? Resisting the top-down powers of the status quo, whether soft or hard, requires siding with alternative powers that tend to move from the bottom up. This is the final way in which travel becomes an act of justice. Solidarity, a word that unfortunately lost its power when well-meaning people claimed it without understanding the flow of power, might come alive again in these situations.[20] The good news, as we have seen, is that there are forms of travel that invite us to side with alternative bottom-up powers. This was the context of many of the Jewish-Christian traditions of old, of the pilgrims of the Middle Ages, of vagabonds who detached themselves from their masters, of religious travelers who seek true relationships with God and with others, and of the many migrants whose primary goal is not to become rich but to make an honest living for their families and for themselves. When we are traveling along these roads, justice may yet become an option.

Notes

PREFACE

[1]Brad Plumer, "Americans still move around more than anyone else in the world," *The Washington Post*, May 13, 2013, www.washingtonpost.com /blogs/wonkblog/wp/2013/05/15/the-united-states-is-still-one-of-the -most-mobile-countries-in-the-world. Accessed March 12, 2015.

CHAPTER 1: THE JUDEO-CHRISTIAN TRADITIONS ON THE ROAD

[1]Frederick Herzog, *God-Walk: Liberation Shaping Dogmatics* (Maryknoll, NY: Orbis, 1988), xi.

[2]See Frederick Herzog, "New Birth of Conscience," in *Liberating the Future: God, Mammon, and Theology*, ed. Joerg Rieger (Minneapolis: Fortress, 1998), 149.

[3]Herzog, *God-Walk*, xiii.

[4]Ibid., xiv.

[5]Homi K. Bhabha, *The Location of Culture* (London: Routledge, 1994), 12.

[6]See Delores S. Williams, *Sisters in the Wilderness: The Challenge of Womanist God-Talk* (Maryknoll, NY: Orbis, 1995).

[7]For an interpretation of the Nicene Creed from the bottom up (that is, from a perspective that takes seriously the life and ministry of Christ on the road), see Joerg Rieger, "Resisting and Reframing Coequality: Christology and the Creeds," in *Christ & Empire: From Paul to Postcolonial Times* (Minneapolis: Fortress, 1997), 69-118.

[8]Norman K. Gottwald, *The Hebrew Bible: A Brief Socio-Literary Introduction* (Minneapolis: Fortress, 2009), 150-57, distinguishes among accounts that interpret the entrance into the Promised Land in terms of conquest, immigration or social revolution. The social-revolution account

combines some of the insights of the other accounts, understanding that the revolution proceeded from the bottom up as various oppressed groups joined forces.

[9]Musa W. Dube and Jeffrey L. Staley, "Descending from and Ascending into Heaven: A Postcolonial Analysis of Travel, Space and Power in John," in *John and Postcolonialism: Travel, Space and Power*, ed. Musa W. Dube and Jeffrey L. Staley (London: Sheffield Academic Press, 2002), 4.

[10]Ibid., 10.

[11]Ibid.

[12]Herzog, *God-Walk*, xxiii.

[13]These terms are used in Jürgen Moltmann, *The Way of Jesus Christ: Christology in Messianic Dimensions*, trans. Margaret Kohl (Minneapolis: Fortress, 1993), xiv. Frederick Herzog talks about a *theologia viatorum* in *God-Walk*, xxiii.

[14]Moltmann, *The Way of Jesus Christ*, xiii.

[15]See Rieger, "Resisting and Reframing Coequality." This is the challenge of and to the Council of Chalcedon.

[16]Herzog, *God-Walk*, xv, xvi.

[17]Steven Vertovec, "Introduction: New directions in the anthropology of migration and multiculturalism," in *Anthropology of Migration and Multiculturalism: New Directions*, ed. Steven Vertovec (London: Routledge, 2010), 2. These developments might have their parallels in theology and religious studies.

[18]James Clifford, "Notes on Travel and Theory," *Inscriptions* 5 (Center for Cultural Studies: 1989), ed. James Clifford and Vivek Dhareshwar, 185.

Chapter 2: Travel, Tourism and Migration

[1]Mark Twain, *The Innocents Abroad, Or: The New Pilgrim's Process* (New York: Oxford University Press, 1996), 650.

[2]Ibid., 646.

[3]Ibid., 647.

[4]In the United States, 16 percent of all working people say they are too busy to take all their vacation days; 20 percent never take vacations. The average vacation time in the United States is thirteen days; in Europe it is forty-two days. Thirty-three percent of Americans check in with their bosses during vacation. See Arthur Asa Berger, *Deconstructing Travel: Cultural Perspectives on Tourism* (Walnut Creek, CA: AltaMira, 2004), 11.

[5]Reference in Freya Higgins-Desbiolles, *Capitalist Globalisation, Corporatised Tourism and their Alternatives* (New York: Nova Science, 2009), 33.

[6]"It is an interesting characteristic of the tourist world that the tourists themselves believe that it has no end, that there is always some new frontier." Dean MacCannell, *The Tourist: A New Theory of the Leisure Class* (New York: Schocken, 1976), 186.

[7]See Kath Weston, *Traveling Light: On the Road with America's Poor* (Boston: Beacon, 2008).

[8]Ibid., xvii.

[9]Ibid., xxi.

[10]Ibid., xx.

[11]Dennison Nash, "Tourism as a Form of Imperialism," in *Hosts and Guests: The Anthropology of Tourism*, second edition, ed. Valene L. Smith (Philadelphia: University of Pennsylvania Press, 1989), 37.

[12]See Edward M. Bruner, "Transformation of Self in Tourism," *Annals of Tourism Research* 18 (1991): 239.

[13]"It is this power over touristic and related developments abroad that makes a metropolitan center imperialistic and tourism a form of imperialism." Nash, "Tourism as a Form of Imperialism," 39.

[14]"All tourists desire this deeper involvement with society and culture to some degree; it is a basic component of their motivation to travel." MacCannell, *The Tourist*, 10.

[15]Roque Planas, "Border Deaths Spike 27 Percent, Even As Immigration from Mexico Drops, Report Says," *The Huffington Post*, March 20, 2013, www.huffingtonpost.com/2013/03/20/border-deaths-spike-27-percent -immigration-mexico_n_2915605.html. Accessed January 28, 2015.

[16]See Christiane Harzig and Dirk Hoerder, with Donna Gabaccia, *What Is Migration History?* (Cambridge, UK: Polity, 2009), 134, 136.

[17]Dean MacCannell, *Empty Meeting Grounds: The Tourist Papers* (London: Routledge, 1992), 2.

[18]Nadje Al-Ali and Khalid Koser, "Transnationalism, International Migration and Home," in *New Approaches to Migration? Transnational Communities and the Transformation of Home*, ed. Nadje Al-Ali and Khalid Koser, Routledge Research in Transnationalism (London: Routledge, 2002), 6.

[19]Ibid., 8.

[20]MacCannell, *Empty Meeting Grounds*, 4-5.

[21]Ibid.

[22]Ibid.

[23]Ibid.

[24]Al-Ali and Koser, "Transnationalism, International Migration and Home," 2.

[25]See also Joerg Rieger and Kwok Pui-lan, *Occupy Religion: Theology of the Multitude*, Religion in the Modern World (Lanham, MD: Rowman & Littlefield, 2012).

Chapter 3: Pilgrims and Vagabonds

[1]Luigi Tomasi, "*Homo Viator*: From Pilgrimages to Religious Tourism via the Journey," in *From Medieval Pilgrimage to Religious Tourism: The Social and Cultural Economics of Piety*, ed. William H. Swatos Jr. and Luigi Tomasi (Westport, CT: Praeger, 2002), 3.

[2]Ellen Badone and Sharon R. Roseman, "Approaches to the Anthropology of Pilgrimage and Tourism," in *Intersecting Journeys: The Anthropology of Pilgrimage and Tourism*, ed. Ellen Badone and Sharon R. Roseman (Urbana: University of Illinois Press, 2004), 2. "Rigid dichotomies between pilgrimage and tourism, or pilgrims and tourists, no longer seem tenable in the shifting world of postmodern travel." Ibid.

[3]Tomasi, "*Homo Viator*," 4. For the following history, see ibid., 4-21.

[4]Ibid., 21.

[5]See Joerg Rieger, "Theology of Difference: The Turn to the Wholly Other," in *God and the Excluded: Visions and Blindspots in Contemporary Theology* (Minneapolis: Fortress, 2001), 43-70.

[6]Badone and Roseman, "Approaches to the Anthropology of Pilgrimage," 3 (reference to Victor Turner).

[7]Walter D. Mignolo, *Local Histories/Global Designs: Coloniality, Subaltern Knowledges, and Border Thinking* (Princeton, NJ: Princeton University Press, 2000).

[8]For the notion of hybridity see Homi K. Bhabha, *The Location of Culture* (London: Routledge, 1994).

[9]"Wir sind nur Gast auf Erden und wandern ohne Ruh mit mancherlei Beschwerden der ewigen Heimat zu. / Die Wege sind verlassen, und oft sind wir allein. In diesen grauen Gassen will niemand bei uns sein. / Nur einer gibt Geleite, das ist der liebe Christ; er wandert treu zur Seite, wenn alles uns vergisst. / Gar manche Wege führen aus dieser Welt hinaus. O, dass wir nicht verlieren, den Weg zum Vaterhaus. / Und sind wir einmal müde,

dann stell ein Licht uns aus, o Gott, in deiner Güte, dann finden wir nach Haus." Georg Thurmair and Adolf Lohmann, 1935/1938, *Gesangbuch der Evangelisch-methodistischen Kirche* (Stuttgart: Medienwerk der Evangelisch-methodistischen Kirche, 2002), 1210. Translation mine.

[10]Zygmunt Bauman, "From Pilgrim to Tourist—or a Short History of Identity," in *Questions of Cultural Identity*, ed. Stuart Hall and Paul du Gay (Los Angeles: SAGE, 1996), 21.

[11]Ibid., 23.

[12]Karl Marx and Friedrich Engels, *The Communist Manifesto* (New York: Pocket, 1964), 63.

[13]Bauman, "From Pilgrim to Tourist," 22.

[14]Ibid., 29. For more on Bauman's notion of the vagabond, see ibid., 26-32. Bauman adds two other types of travelers: strollers walk among strangers as stranger, and their relationships remain on the surface. The shopping mall is their habitat, where strolling is safe and without consequence, similar to watching TV. Strolling is noncommittal, with no challenge to private lives and the status quo. Players live in a world of risks and need to manage those risks. Yet everything is merely a game. The other becomes an object of aesthetic rather than moral evaluation, a matter of taste rather than responsibility. Their only concerns are whether something is "interesting" and whether it provides enjoyment.

[15]The title of the song is "Es, es, es und es." The original text of the stanza: "Ich sag es ihm frei ins Gesicht: sein Lohn und seine Arbeit gefall'n mir nicht. Ich will mein Glück probieren, marschieren."

[16]John Leland, *Why Kerouac Matters: The Lessons of* On the Road *(They're Not What You Think)* (New York: Viking, 2007), 68.

[17]Jack Kerouac, *On the Road* (New York: Penguin, 2003), 5-6.

[18]Ibid., 19.

[19]John Steinbeck, *Travels with Charley: In Search of America* (New York: Penguin, 1986), 6.

[20]"People identify things only in context." Ibid., 7.

[21]The sentences immediately before this quotation read, "Once a journey is designed, equipped, and put in process; a new factor enters and takes over. A trip, a safari, an exploration, is an entity, different from all other journeys. It has personality, temperament, individuality, uniqueness. . . . And all plans, safeguards, policing, and coercion are fruitless." Ibid., 4.

[22]Ibid., 20.

[23]Ibid., 277.

[24]Lois Pryce, *Lois on the Loose: One Woman, One Motorcycle, 20,000 Miles Across the Americas* (New York: Thomas Dunne, 2007), 293.

[25]Ibid.

[26]Dave Barr with Mike Wourms, *Riding the Edge: An 83,000 Mile Motorcycle Adventure Around the World!* (Bodfish, CA: Dave Barr Publications, 1999).

[27]Ernesto Che Guevara, *The Motorcycle Diaries: Notes on a Latin American Journey* (London: Harper Perennial, 2003), 79.

[28]Ibid., 119.

[29]Ibid., 32.

[30]Ibid., 164.

[31]Patrick Symmes, *Chasing Che: A Motorcycle Journey in Search of the Guevara Legend* (New York: Vintage, 2000), 10.

[32]Robert M. Pirsig, *Zen and the Art of Motorcycle Maintenance: An Inquiry into Values* (New York: Morrow, 1984).

[33]Rolf Potts, *Vagabonding: An Uncommon Guide to the Art of Long-Term World Travel* (New York: Villard, 2003), 5.

[34]Paul Fussell, *Abroad*, quoted in Potts, *Vagabonding*, 92, without page reference.

[35]Potts, *Vagabonding*, 109.

[36]Reference in ibid., 119.

[37]See, for instance, David Elliot Cohen, *One Year Off: Leaving It All Behind for a Round-the-World Journey with Our Children* (San Francisco: Travelers' Tales, 2001).

[38]Charles Kuralt, *A Life on the Road*, quoted in Potts, *Vagabonding*, 178, without publication data.

[39]Potts, *Vagabonding*, 190.

Chapter 4: Beyond Religious Tourism

[1]See, for instance, Philip Jenkins, *The New Faces of Christianity: Believing the Bible in the Global South* (Oxford, UK: Oxford University Press, 2006).

[2]See Joerg Rieger, "Theology and Mission Between Neocolonialism and Postcolonialism," *Mission Studies: Journal of the International Association for Mission Studies* 21, no. 2 (2004): 201-27.

[3]For a discussion of these problems, see Brian M. Howell, "That's No Missionary!" in *Short-Term Mission: An Ethnography of Christian Travel Narrative and Experience* (Downers Grove, IL: IVP Academic, 2012), 69-86.

[4]David Harvey, *The Condition of Postmodernity: An Enquiry into the Origins of Cultural Change* (Oxford, UK: Blackwell, 1990), 351.

[5]Susan B. Thistlethwaite and George F. Cairns, eds., *Beyond Theological Tourism: Mentoring as a Grassroots Approach to Theological Education* (Maryknoll, NY: Orbis, 1994).

[6]Marji Bishir, "El Salvador Habitat project provides two-way lessons," *United Methodist Reporter*, December 8, 2010, www.ntcumc.org/news /detail/1775.

[7]See, for instance, George Tinker, *Missionary Conquest: The Gospel and Native American Genocide* (Minneapolis: Fortress, 1993), who tells the story of the missionaries to the Native Americans in this fashion.

[8]Susan Thistlethwaite, "Beyond Theological Tourism," in Thistlethwaite and Cairns, *Beyond Theological Tourism*, 14.

[9]Ibid., 12.

[10]This is a variant on Gayatri Spivak's famous question whether the subaltern can speak, which has shaped the history of postcolonial theory. While Spivak initially denied the possibility, she later noted that this question depends on the situation. See Gayatri Chakravorty Spivak, *A Critique of Postcolonial Reason: Toward a History of the Vanishing Present* (Cambridge, MA: Harvard University Press, 1999), 306-9. More important, it seems to me, is the fact that we consider the speaking of the subaltern as ongoing efforts.

[11]Phaedra C. Pezzullo, *Toxic Tourism: Rhetorics of Pollution, Travel, and Environmental Justice* (Tuscaloosa: University of Alabama Press, 2007), 1-2.

[12]Ibid., 3.

[13]Ibid., 10.

[14]Keep in mind that German fascism killed six million Jews in its concentration camps, but also six million others, including socialists, communists, labor leaders, gays and lesbians, gypsies and people with disabilities.

[15]Historian Dagobert Runes, quoted in Rolf Potts, *Vagabonding: An Uncommon Guide to the Art of Long-Term World Travel* (New York: Villard, 2003), 116, without data.

[16]This is the summary of Bonhoeffer's biographer and close friend, Eberhard Bethge. See Eberhard Bethge, *Dietrich Bonhoeffer: Man of Vision, Man of Courage* (New York: Harper, 1970), 771.

[17]Dietrich Bonhoeffer, *Letters and Papers from Prison*, ed. Eberhard Bethge (New York: Touchstone, 1997), 17.

Chapter 5: Travel as an Act of Justice

[1]Rick Steves, *Travel as Political Act* (New York: Nation, 2009), 96-97.

[2]For historical examples of how empire is manifest in both soft and hard power, see Joerg Rieger, *Globalization and Theology*, Horizons in Theology (Nashville: Abingdon, 2010).

[3]For the remaining fragments, see Friedrich Daniel Ernst Schleiermacher, "Materialien zur Siedlungsgeschichte Neuhollands (Australiens)," in *Schriften aus der Berliner Zeit 1800–1802*, ed. Günter Meckenstock, *Kritische Gesamtausgabe*, ed. Hans-Joachim Birkner et al., abt. 1, vol. 3 (Berlin: de Gruyter, 1988).

[4]For the background of the following account, see Joerg Rieger, "Resisting and Reframing Prophet, Priest, and King: Christology and Later Colonialism," in *Christ & Empire: From Paul to Postcolonial Times* (Minneapolis: Fortress, 1997), 197-236.

[5]See Kwok Pui-lan, *Postcolonial Imagination and Feminist Theology* (Louisville: Westminster John Knox, 2005), 194.

[6]Dean MacCannell, *Empty Meeting Grounds: The Tourist Papers* (London: Routledge, 1992), 1.

[7]Reference in Freya Higgins-Desbiolles, *Capitalist Globalisation, Corporatised Tourism and their Alternatives* (New York: Nova Science, 2009), 33.

[8]Ibid., 48.

[9]This is the General Agreement on Trade in Services (GATS), paralleling free-trade agreements. Ibid., 52. The GATS's "national treatment clause" requires that foreign corporations will receive the same treatment as domestic companies. Ibid., 53. In addition, exceptions can be granted. In 2000, the United States requested removal of regulations having to do with the need to repatriate profits, employment of locals, support for local businesses, and restrictions on sale or rent of property and on share of foreign investment. Ibid., 54.

[10]See ibid., 80, 84.

[11]Frederick J. Ruf, *Bewildered Travel: The Sacred Quest for Confusion* (Charlottesville: University of Virginia Press, 2007), 4.

[12]Ibid., 5, 8 (the reference to love of ruptures), 189-90.

[13]Most interpreters are now agreed on the centrality of the covenant and of relationship in the understanding of the biblical notions of justice. See, e.g., Christopher D. Marshall, *Beyond Retribution: A New Testament Vision for*

Justice, Crime, and Punishment (Grand Rapids: Eerdmans, 2001); and Walter Kerber, Claus Westermann, and Bernhard Spörlein, "Gerechtigkeit," in *Christlicher Glaube in moderner Gesellschaft,* Teilband 17 (Freiburg, Germany: Herder, 1981).

[14]See the Jewish theologian Moshe Weinfeld, "'Justice and Righteousness': The Expression and its Meaning," in *Justice and Righteousness: Biblical Themes and Their Influence,* ed. Henning Graf Reventlow and Yair Hoffman (Sheffield, UK: Sheffield Academic Press, 1992), 238.

[15]K. Koch, "sdq, gemeinschaftstreu/heilvoll sein," in *Theologisches Handwörterbuch zum Alten Testament,* ed. Ernst Jenni and Claus Westermann (Munich and Zurich: Christian Kaiser Verlag, Theologischer Verlag Zürich, 1984), 2:507-30.

[16]Dieter Lührmann, "Gerechtigkeit III," in *Theologische Realenzyklopädie,* ed. Gerhard Krause and Gerhard Müller (Berlin: Walter de Gruyter, 1984), 12:419.

[17]See Elsa Tamez, *The Amnesty of Grace: Justification by Faith from a Latin American Perspective,* trans. Sharon H. Ringe (Nashville: Abingdon, 1993).

[18]That was the point of my book *God and the Excluded: Visions and Blindspots in Contemporary Theology* (Minneapolis: Fortress, 2001).

[19]John Wesley, "Upon Our Lord's Sermon on the Mount, Eleventh Discourse," in *The Bicentennial Edition of the Works of John Wesley,* ed. Albert C. Outler (Nashville: Abingdon, 1984), 1:672.

[20]See also my notion of "deep solidarity," for instance, in Joerg Rieger and Kwok Pui-lan, *Occupy Religion: Theology of the Multitude,* Religion in the Modern World (Lanham, MD: Rowman & Littlefield, 2012).

Subject Index

Finding the Textbook You Need

The IVP Academic Textbook Selector
is an online tool for instantly finding the IVP books
suitable for over 250 courses across 24 disciplines.

ivpacademic.com